RESTORED &
Remarried

Restored & Remarried

Remarried

ENCOURAGEMENT FOR REMARRIED COUPLES IN A STEPFAMILY

Seven Trees Media

GIL & BRENDA STUART

Seven Trees Media

A Publication of Seven Trees Media
Vancouver, WA | USA 360-904-2117 | www.seventreesmedia.com

Cover art by Katie Bredemeier.
Design and layout by Michelle DeMonnin, DeMonnin's Art Studio, Inc.
for Burck Communications, www.burckcommunications.com
Photo of Gil and Brenda Stuart by Niccole W Photography, Vancouver, WA

All Scripture quotations, unless otherwise indicated, are taken from the Ryrie Study Bible,
New American Standard Translation, Copyright 1976, 1978 by the Moody Bible Institute.
Used by permission. All rights reserved.

Copyright © 2009 by Gil and Brenda Stuart.
Seven Trees Media | Vancouver, WA | USA 360-904-2117 | www.seventreesmedia.com

ISBN: 978-0-557-10852-7

Printed in the United States of America. All rights reserved under International Copyright
Law. Contents and/or cover may not be reproduced in whole or in part in any form without
the express written consent of the publisher.

This book is *lovingly* dedicated to "Those People" in order of their age: Joshua, Joel, Daniel, Kyle, Patrick, Kara, and Jeffrey.

RESTORED & Remarried

Contents

RESTORED &
Remarried

Acknowledgements

Taking into account the scores of people and resources that have made this book possible, finding the right words of gratitude is a huge task. As silly as it sounds, we begin by recognizing our former spouses.

Yes, you got it right. We wish to thank each of them for the lessons learned, the knowledge gained, and the good years enjoyed. When our divorces occurred, the aches and sorrows all of us endured seemed to take center stage. Everyone lost something…or everything. No one escapes a divorce without scars. However, there were lots of mutually sustaining experiences during the good years and these must be acknowledged at the onset of a book about remarriage.

Surely our former spouses will be our toughest critics. Rightfully so! They, like us, made choices during our respective divorces that were heart wrenching and painful for all involved. To ignore this fact would be an atrocity and would be disrespectful to them—regardless of the why's, what's, or who's involved.

Backtracking at times cannot be avoided, but now our attitude is a determined one of "Always forward!" Getting on with life is now the order of the day!

RESTORED & *Remarried*

We must also start this book by thanking our children as well. Thank you, kids, for your expressions of love and acceptance to us even when you were angry, confused, or sorting out how not to betray your own hearts. We want you to know we try to understand your position in how you relate to us now. We love you and are proud to be your mom/stepmom and dad/stepdad.

We also wish to encourage you in your futures by saying we are so sorry you have to travel the road of being from a broken family. Our hope is that as you journey through life you will know we love each of you, now from the context of a blended family. Although we cannot change the past, we trust that your legacy will have the stability it needs from a foundation of forgiveness toward the adults you call "Mom" and "Dad."

During the turbulent times of our divorces, there were people who helped us and kept us upright when we felt that our world was falling apart…because it was! The hours spent trying to "figure it out" took people with open hearts, open ears, and a lot of patience. Those we chose to bare our hearts to were solid, down-to-earth folks who steered us to the cross of Christ. They helped us accept and forgive ourselves for the losses, as well as for our own shortcomings.

Personally the list for me (Gil) would be a mile long, but to name a few would be guys like Craig Hansen, Scott Smith, Doug Crane, Joe Anfuso, Dave Galanter, E.C. Wilson, Marty Martinez, Darrel Henry, and all the guys in my small groups at the time.

Brenda's special thanks would list Tom and Shawn Perez, Kathy Rohrer, Chris and Laura Kast, Joan Smith, Robin and Steve Esposito, Dave Galanter, Bruce and Vicky Dillon, Traci Ausborn, and Lori Wooster.

The day came when a new relationship between Brenda and me began to grow. There were key individuals who walked us through the process. Even if the interaction was once or twice, their counsel was rich and full of grace. Keeping ourselves accountable and influenced by each of these people gave the foundation of our marriage a firm reality check to our commitment. Thank you to all the following—we would not be here if not for your love and encouragement: Bob and Sally Walton, Carl and Tami LaCasse, Alan Sanders, Grace (Raub) Quartson,

Lydia Budai, Steve Hotra, and Mark and Lynn Miller (the "husband 20 questions test" will live in our memory forever), and the whole staff at Summit View Church (Dave and Chris—you know who you are).

During that time, we also relied upon authors who we would later meet in person: Ron Deal, Drs. Les and Leslie Parrott, Moe and Paige Becnel, and Maxine and Charlie Marsolini. Thank you all.

Karla Dornacher, we wish to express a special thanks for encouraging us to write to those couples we will never meet or who will never have opportunity to join in a Restored and Remarried seminar.

Great encouragers through our marriage work in the Northwest and beyond are: Jeff Kemp and Luke Nelson from Stronger Families, and K. Jason Krafsky and the fellow board members of Thriving Families of Clark County, Mark, Dave, Al, Brad, Dennis, and Jim.

We traveled to many special places to work on this project. Terry and Shirley Wollam's beach house, Bruce and Vicky's lake house, Dan and Susan Gauger's beach house, Tony Tuck's prayer cabin, and Beacon Rock State Park! Thanks to all who made those getaways possible.

Thank you too, to our incredible team at Burck Communications: Bradley, Moriah, Jay, Devin and Michelle. Your encouragement and patient guidance has been invaluable.

We get the adventure, God gets the glory!

"God will fix a fix to fix you, and if you wiggle out of that fix, He'll fix another to fix you."

—Arthur L. Stuart, third generation rancher, Frasier, Idaho

Introduction

Why Did We Write This Book?

No one plans for a catastrophe; it just happens to you! After the catastrophe, it's up to you to make your way through the aftermath the best you can, with or without instructions. Neither of us thought we would ever be in such a situation as we've come to call the "great train wreck" (aka "divorce"). It was such a tragedy! Long-term marriages (23 years for Gil and 19 years for Brenda), with adult children as well as young children in their formative years, were thrown into a state of upheaval.

By definition, to be remarried means one has divorced or been widowed then married a second time (or more). There were good years. Your children and family life experiences contributed to who you are to some extent now, so reflect as positively as you can on those experiences. Bad years tend to overshadow good, and a divorce, as anyone who has been through that mess can tell you, wipes out anything that was worth holding onto.

An unexpected death is filled with grief, yet a person can reflect on the positives through the grieving process. Whereas with the death of a marriage, the grief lives on so it is important to take the proper steps to grieve and "conclude" the past.

At the time of our divorces we were "in the church," so we thought these things weren't supposed to be happening to us. We're supposed to be insulated from stuff like that, right? You guessed it, we weren't. Maybe we were just naïve? I (Gil) felt bulletproof to the epidemic of divorce that pervades the world and the church.

Before my own divorce, I (Gil) had a certain attitude toward people who went through divorce within the church community. Truthfully, I was confused about how that could be happening to people if they had the insulation of being in the church. I would question, "Did they sin or blow it somehow?" In my judgmental opinion (as limited as it was at the time), I just did not get what the problems were that would unravel a loving marriage.

Meeting someone new may not have been on your radar or finding a potential mate could be a priority early after your divorce. To establish healthy, new, genuine friendships and connecting with that "just right person" after a divorce, you need to be done dealing with your past stuff. Then when your paths cross with someone special you are prepared to offer a "whole you" again. Personally I (Gil) am not a big fan of dating services or computer matching surveys. As Brenda and I each set out on new directions for our lives individually, post divorces, our paths crossed.

We were friends at first, able to understand and support each other because of our common experience. Then after a year's time and lots of talking, we decided to take the step toward another marriage. Immediately, we went looking for resources. They were few and far between. We found only a few books and some articles, but no hands-on classes or workshops to attend locally. After marriage, we traveled to a conference in another state to learn about the unique challenges of remarriage and struggles that blended families face.

You've heard the stories, statistics, and challenges that face remarried couples today. Situations encountered daily bring home the dynamics of remarriage and stepfamilies. Current studies of our society reveal that **one out of three** people are affected in some way by divorce and remarriage.[1]

Sixty percent of second marriages result in divorce before the second year of the marriage.[2] A key component to this is the lack of restoration from the first divorce. Restoration is for the one being left, as well as the one doing the leaving. Restoration is available equally. Healing comes from the act of forgiveness. Forgiveness is experienced ultimately by the human heart through the work of grace provided by Christ's redemption.

Having a second marriage to openly enjoy companionship and closeness was a gift we never expected. When we chose to say "I do" for the second time, we wanted a plan that would sustain us when the going got tough. Because we knew it *would* get tough. It's hard work to have a good marriage, but to have a great marriage, all the more effort is required. We knew we'd need special insight to succeed in a remarriage. Resources written from the heart by couples who had frontline experience dealing specifically with remarriage were few to none.

Marriage is an incredible gift that people take for granted. Often the vows have boiled down to "until divorce do us part." A life-long commitment designed to bring joy, safety, and adventure is under tremendous attack. The intent is never to divorce. That would be insane or downright stupid! Who in their right mind would purposefully direct their lives into one of the most destructive and painful experiences of life? More insane would be to go through such an event a second or third time!

Many people we have talked with at our seminars have not done their homework about remarriage. They feel that they have been married before and understand marriage. We ask them, "How's that working for you?" They are not anticipating being blindsided by issues they did not foresee or are unique to remarriage. They find themselves talking about divorce again. It is scary to think that many view divorce as an optional remedy to their troubles.

RESTORED & *Remarried*

As we have grown through our remarriage experience, we have created communication methods that have helped us navigate these waters. Because these skills have saved us from enormous hurts and miscommunication, we want to share them with others. We've found from presenting our seminar, Restored and Remarried, that what is working for us works for others.

What an incredible honor it has been to come alongside other remarried couples and see relationships restored, and marriages and families thrive.

Remarriage is marriage, but has distinctive obstacles with unseen ghosts of past emotions and habits. Taking the steps to deal with past habits and to heal old hurts is vital to the restoration of each individual. It's also an important part of starting over.

It's not just about you or just about the marriage anymore; it's about the kids too (if you have any). Bringing together different traditions, rules, and personalities from two different families is no picnic. It's not easy, but it can work, and work quite well. It takes trust, honesty, and commitment to give the stepfamily process a chance to succeed. It requires a "no turning back" attitude. Do you want them to go through another divorce? In most situations, your kids never even asked for the remarriage in the first place.

There is one common thread that weaves throughout our seminars, workshops, and writings: *If you ain't got the marriage, you ain't got nothin'!* Meaning, the family will be as strong as the marriage. The health, vitality, and desired longevity of the current primary relationships within the family makes the marriage key.

Avoid another divorce; get your current marriage into focus! We want to help!

We have been conducting Restored and Remarried seminars since 2005, sharing our experiences and what we've learned from them with couples who are considering remarriage or have been "blending their family" for years. Now we are compiling the teaching of these seminars into this book—in order to reach and help even more couples and families. We are going to share what happens when two marriages, spanning three decades, dissolve, throwing seven children from age ten to early twenties into confusion. That confusion is then compounded when two people (their parents) choose to love again and get remarried!

When asked how long we've been married we share the actual number of years, which is six (as of the time of writing this book). But we like to do the "remarried math" for people as well. Here is how it works:

Take the combined number of children that you have, then multiply that by the years married. So in our case that is 7 kids x 6 years married = 42 years. When you do the math this way it is a far more accurate measurement of time because of the intensity of life with the blending factor of "those people" combined in a short amount of time. ("Those people" is our term for the kids involved in a blended family. We are always asking, "What are 'those people' doing? When will 'those people' clean up after themselves? When are 'those people' leaving?") We love all of our children and they do bring color to our life!

In this book we share lessons from our own stepfamily adventure. We share heart-to-heart as we walk the walk. Is it always easy? No! We can see why people don't like to speak or write about this topic. It conjures up so much pain. But the Lord in His mercy has put it on our hearts to be your encouragers and your loudest cheerleaders.

Being a resource is our passion! In a way, we've come looking for you to share what has helped us, and then learn together how to strengthen, enrich, and protect what we all have now. Sharing our "guts and glory" stories can strengthen us, not the fables of some sitcom TV show. We believe that helping you know you are not alone in modern stepfamily life will make a difference for the good of all.

Applying Restored and Remarried concepts begins with you! Sharing the benefits with others promotes the principles of R & R first at your house, then throughout the future of your kids, and eventually your whole community!

The fact that you picked up this book is evidence you want more for your remarriage than what you have right now! As you begin to read, keep in mind the common thread:

"If you ain't got the marriage,

you ain't got nothin.'"

—Gil and Brenda Stuart, Authors, Encouragers,
and "Happily Remarried"

"Love is seeking to act for

the other person's highest good."

—Jerry Cook

Chapter 1

Restored Foundations, Adjusted Expectations, and Misleading Myths

Chapter 1

Restored Foundations, Adjusted Expectations, and Misleading Myths

Current studies of our society reveal that one out of three people is affected in some way by divorce and remarriage.[1] In addition, studies show that 60 percent of second marriages result in divorce before the second year of the marriage.[2] A key component of this is the lack of restoration. Restoration is needed both for the one being left, as well as for the one doing the leaving. Restoration is available to each spouse equally.

The first step of restoration is repentance. Please don't confuse that concept with just being a religious term. Repentance is an action based in the process of forgiveness that all can understand. In simple terms it is a change of mind, a change in direction, an about face. The beauty of this choice is that once I take that step, Jesus meets me right there

with the repairs for my soul and emotions like no other person or drug or material gadget can do. Your self-worth is now restored. You have a new foundation that is whole, and if you are willing, you are able to be offered to a new spouse.

We believe the next step toward restoration is found in authentic forgiveness. Forgiveness does not dismiss wrong action. The best example of such forgiveness is found in the actions of Jesus. Jesus offered us forgiveness despite our wrong actions and continued unrighteous attitudes toward Him and others.

> *Real change by God's grace is normal, just not common.*

Now I know we cannot measure up to His standard, but accepting that He can work forgiveness into our character through faith is a great relief. Healing comes from the act of forgiveness. Forgiveness is experienced ultimately by the human heart through the work of grace provided by Christ's redemption.

There are two points needing clarification when you move this principle of forgiveness into real life situations. First, you need to apply forgiveness to yourself; and second, forgiveness should be extended to your former spouse. In some cases the forgiveness you extend to your former spouse may be rejected, and your request for his or her forgiveness may be denied. You may instead be met with more blame piled on you. Whatever happens with your gesture of forgiveness, be genuine. Extend and seek forgiveness anyway, because it is the only key out of a prison of bitterness, anger, or hurt. And being free of all those burdens is required to be wholehearted in your new marriage.

The final step toward restoration is change. To extend forgiveness without demanding change or to accept forgiveness without moving toward change makes the grace Jesus extends to you a sham or an accomplice to more evil. If you don't deal with accepting change provided by grace, you are abusing the gift of grace. You're just asking for more evil, more selfishness, more wrong actions and wrong attitudes to breed in your life, which affects everyone around you. You have neutered the power of God's grace by not acting upon it with real change. Real change by God's grace is normal, just not common. Change is the divine tool in the hands of Jesus in the life of the believer. Repentance, to put it another way to emphasize the importance, is having godly sorrow for our actions and then choosing to turn and walk in a new direction and way of life.

Tough Questions

To begin to move forward with an understanding of forgiveness, ask yourself the following tough questions. (To help you with a starting point for your discussion, we have included our own conversation we had about these tough questions.) Don't edit your reply. Blurt out your answers honestly. Once you've done that, apply the forgiveness principle or take the steps required to respond to your gut reaction, or find the resources necessary to finish the business of your heart's aspiration.

1. **Did you learn or grow from your mistake or mishap from your previous marriage?**

   Gil: Yeah, that was tough because I had to deal with personal issues that I had ignored or actions that I could have done better, then be certain not to repeat those mistakes again. Rather than place blame on my ex-wife, I had to take personal responsibility internally and then accept my failures. After that step, I found forgiveness first for myself and then could begin the healing.

   Brenda: As I took time to reflect on my part of "the great train wreck" I grew personally. I wanted to make sure that the one positive thing I could take from my divorce was becoming a better person. I wanted to lighten my load of baggage that has weighed me down through life; being able to separate the lies from the truths about who I was as a person, and who I wanted to be.

2. **Do you experience confusion/shame as being part of an alternative family?**

Gil: Definitely! I was confused by trying to learn how to love and accept my new kids, let alone how to make my new wife comfortable. As a churchgoer I felt like I was second rate and ashamed of the fallout of being divorced no matter whose fault it was. I did not want to be recognized in that crowd, so it was tough to acknowledge for awhile when people would ask about my family, past or present. It was awkward to say I had stepkids.

Brenda: Yes, I did early on. I felt—like many people do—that I needed to keep up a façade or my Sunday-best face (especially at church). I wanted to fit in and look like a normal traditional family. I wanted to look that way, but was torn apart inside with unaddressed feelings of shame and guilt. I had a judgmental spirit against stepfamilies before my divorce, and then there I was, in the same situation I had judged others. God really broke me of that mind-set.

3. **Do your wounds transfer to your kids?**

Gil: I am certain they do because each one in his/her own way deals with the pain and scars that were inflicted upon them out of no fault of their own. Plus, my hurt and disappointment in the loss of our family took me so low that often the kids were sad that I was sad. It has taken years now for them to be able to talk about it and have a good cry together. Some of my kids still, I think, are hurting. It is difficult for them to deal with the pain it has caused them.

Brenda: I tried the best I could to separate my feelings toward my ex from my kids. They did not need to carry the burden and hurt I felt; they had their own hurts to deal with. As good of a job as I think I did at not transferring my wounds, it is never 100 percent. Thank goodness for an open relationship and the concept of

forgiveness. I did my best to have my kids see how Christ carried me through the tough times.

4.   **Do you have a safe place to talk?**

Gil: Yes, finding a group of godly men was one of the first things I sought out while I was going through the divorce. Each man I found was someone safe with whom to share my heart. I knew that their counsel would be honest, encouraging, and wise, even if I did not always like their suggestions. Maintaining a safe place between Brenda and myself now is built on having a group of men I know I can turn to for prayer, counsel, and accountability.

Brenda: I didn't really understand what a safe place meant until this relationship. I understand now that the strongest, best relationships are built on safety and trust as their foundations. If I don't feel safe, how can I share where I am really at? Is it scary? You bet. Is it worth it? I wouldn't have it any other way. I feel safe to talk with Gil.

5.   **Remarriage/stepfamily resources are few. Did you research and review or just jump in?**

Gil: I was a sponge, reading anything I could find about divorce and remarriage. I was very fortunate to find Brenda! She is all about gathering information and applying what she learns to real life. We found a few books and workbooks together that provided information, as well as excellent questions, motives, and character traits of remarriage and stepfamily life. We found seminars and marriage enrichment materials that dealt with the issues of marriage as well as remarriage.

Brenda: Many people we have encountered thought, "Hey, I've been married before; this will be the same." Boy, how wrong can they be? The second or even third time around is a whole new ball game. It is so important to gather information so you can make good decisions and understand what's REALLY going on, especially in your heart.

Redemption

After a divorce and remarriage, many people sometimes get the impression from society—and even from our churches—that remarried couples/blended families are second-rate citizens or Christians. That is IMPOSSIBLE, because there is no such thing as a first-rate citizen or Christian.

Divorce and remarriage are far more acceptable in society and modern culture today than they used to be. Nonetheless, feelings of failure do not go away. Men and women who enjoyed being husband and wife, then later experience a divorce, can't avoid the crushing aftereffects. Approximately 90 percent of divorcées choose to remarry. Hopefully, both individuals have dealt with their past failures, in order to avoid carrying those faults into a new marriage relationship.

We know that when couples come to an R&R seminar, some have accepted Jesus Christ and others have not. But they all have a desire to gain relationship skills and principles to make a better go of the new marriage they are in or will soon be entering. We know the same is true of the readers of this book. It is important to have a working knowledge of redemption to build upon. To have an understanding of God's redemption, Romans 3:23 and 24 is used as a biblical reference:

> *verse 23*   *". . . for all have sinned and fallen short of the glory of God . . ."*

> *verse 24*   *". . . being justified as a gift by His grace through the redemption which is in Christ Jesus."*

What does redemption mean? Taking out all the "christianese," Webster's Dictionary defines redemption as:

- to buy back, or win back

- to release from blame or debt

- to change for the better

- to repair, restore

- to make worthwhile

With these points being made, let's ask ourselves some questions:

1. **Has God released and forgiven you for leaving or being left in your last marriage?**

   The answer is, yes!

> *Has God released and forgiven you for leaving or being left in your last marriage?*

2. **Have you accepted God's forgiveness? Have you been able to embrace the pain, and then allow that same pain to work out godly sorrow?**

   Once you begin the process, however difficult it is, to face off with the pain, then real healing can begin based on an attitude of forgiveness and true maturity.

3. **Have you forgiven yourself for the harm that you have brought on your children and family?**

   I (Gil) think for me this is the toughest issue to face off with because the part that I contributed to the "great train wreck" is for a lifetime. My response to my former spouse when the divorce hit home was, "What about the kids?" What about the birthdays, the graduations, the new babies, and events that families look forward to sharing? These events now would become more stressful because

we would not be sharing them as an intact family.

Don't get me wrong here, when these events occur we enjoy them to the fullest. In the context of a blended family the circumstances can get awkward depending on how the forgiveness factor has been established. For the most part, some events get shared with everyone together in the family and other times an event is celebrated in each separate home. The kid is the focus, but sorry to say, it's still less than what any of us really hoped for when our first families were forming.

So, to answer the question, "Have you forgiven yourself for the harm that you have brought on your children and family?" It does boil down to doing business with the pain and disappointment as quickly and thoroughly as possible. Trust me, this particular issue does not go away, but it does become manageable emotionally if you use the key of forgiveness each time you encounter guilt or shame.

4. **Have you been freed from the shame of a failed relationship (even co-habitating) and/or failed marriage?**

This question really demands an honest look into your soul to know the answer. If the shame or guilt is still there, then the forgiveness factor most likely has not been applied earnestly for yourself yet. As illustrated by faulty construction of a building, if the foundation is not squared away, the more you build, the clearer the defect becomes. Give yourself a break here. The rhythm of your heart and gut instincts can be trusted if aligned with relational truths. Relational truths can be found in resources by authors such as John Gottman and Gary Smalley, as well as from several great principles in the Bible that apply to life as well. Go avail yourself of solid materials that you can relate to and then put them into practice. Get healthy and get free to live with a whole heart once again.

5. **Have you trusted God in His redemptive power and honestly applied that to your own life first?**

Honestly, have you got a grip on this point yet? Take redemption seriously with as much faith as you have in the chair you are sitting in. Then you will see change. Restoration that is authentic and lasts is seen in people who get this issue of redemption resolved once and for all. In our western culture we have become so learned, educated, researched, and documented that our heart's ability to breathe the fresh air of truth is stifled with data.

Great relationships are usually all or nothing propositions. The halfhearted ones that are lived for personal convenience are not built to last and are rarely satisfying for very long. Ask yourself here: "Has the forgiveness factor penetrated my heart and way of thinking fully?" You desire restoration and a happy new marriage or you would not be reading this book or willingly coming to a Restored and Remaried seminar. So what are you waiting for?

You are invited by a loving Savior named Jesus Christ to accept His forgiveness and grace. He invites you into a new life for the first time or to recommit to Him. If you would chose to do so, please do the following: share your decision with another believer, then have them pray with you. Email us (brenda@restoredandremarried. com) and tell us your story of getting this point squared away as another step in your restoration.

> *God gives the power,*
> *I surrender to the process.*

Restoration will be an ongoing process as you experience healing, growth, and enjoyment in your new marriage. Take a look at the following diagram. It is a model of the process of dealing with God's redemption:

- Confession is my part.

- Redemption is God's part.

- Repentance is where confession and redemption come together.

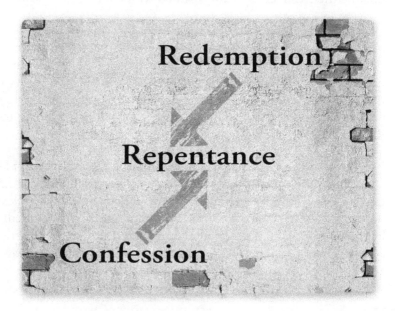

Contradiction

After sharing the previous illustration, we'll now pose a complete contradiction which needs a bit of background to understand. Mark Gungor (author of *Laugh Your Way to a Better Marriage*) was the featured speaker at the Clark County Mayors' Prayer Breakfast in our county. With his good humor and challenges to the audience, Mark made a startling statement that we both agreed and disagreed with at the same time. He said:

> *"You don't have to have God in your marriage to have a successful marriage."* [3]

He explained that if you drop a rock, it falls down due to the natural law of gravity. Like gravity, similar rules apply to relationships that include marriage. If relationship rules such as respect, honesty, unselfishness, love, and acceptance are followed, you can count on the relationship to be successful. Therefore, you don't have to have God in your marriage to have a successful marriage. Just because you slap a Jesus label on your marriage, it does not mean that you are immune to problems or that you can break the rules of relationship gravity.

Don't get us wrong here, God makes it easier to have a good relationship, but the DNA of relationships in great marriages is trust and honesty. But if you look around, the human race doesn't have those two things down too well. Trust and honesty in our society have been reduced to "what feels good—do it." Another mode of situational ethics is to justify our actions. The real killer is self-gratification: "I want what I want right now!"

Ladies and gentlemen, look around. Who and what allowed these viruses to come in to destroy trust and honesty in your previous relationship? Was it you or your ex-spouse? Who and what broke, bruised, burned, buried, or blew up your ability to trust and be honest? It may not have been in your first marriage; it may have been in your family of origin. Was trust and honesty broken by your mom, dad, aunt, uncle, an abusive situation, neglect, or ignorance? What was it?

> *The cure for the pain is in the pain.*

When you can identify it and get that in the open, you can receive restoration. For me (Gil) it was a choice to run toward the pain rather than to run from the pain. As a pastor friend of mine put it to me at the time, "The cure for the pain is in the pain." Embracing difficult painful

experiences and allowing the issues to have their impact sounds totally backwards. Mind you, I had pastoral care and a men's accountability group around me every step of the way so as not to do the process alone and drift into unhealthy conclusions about myself.

Once you have begun this process of restoration, then you can begin to strengthen your remarriage and your relationship with your kids. But first you have to get real with yourself in every dimension of life. As I like to describe it, you need to be spiritually, emotionally, and relationally nude. That's where God makes it easier. Can you trust Him to rescue you from one of the greatest train wrecks called divorce?

Listen in to a discussion Brenda and I had early on in our relationship.

Trust and Honesty

Brenda: "This whole trust and honesty thing can sound so theoretical and irrelevant. I am a detailed, application person. How does trust and honesty have anything to do with our daily circumstances? What if I have an issue with one of your kids, how does trust and honesty help me?"

> *God never moves out of our lives...*

Gil: "If we practice trust and honesty in our marriage, and we have truly experienced it, and are holding ourselves to those principles, we'll be able to pass that on in our relationships with our kids. When trust and honesty are absent, it creates interference and barriers in our relationship. Issues with your ex-husband or my ex-wife, being protective and defensive about kids, or how to deal with your mom, all have to be dealt with in an atmosphere of trust and honesty. [This last point about my mother-in-law is said with humor and respect!] But, if trust and honesty in the marriage have a strong foundation, we will be able to communicate and work through any issue. This won't be easy, yet it'll be worth the effort."

We don't want just a good marriage, we want a GREAT marriage.

Brenda: This was a real conversation we had. At the beginning of our relationship we basically said if we can't have trust and honesty here, well, it was nice knowing you and have a good life. (We literally shook hands in agreement.) After we were married, we shared with our kids that we wanted trust and honesty as the foundation for our family.

Gil: We agreed that trust and honesty would help change the tide of the legacy of our family. They are key to strengthening the future for the hope and health of the whole family. Circumstances of all kinds have tested our commitment to this concept, and we know the more we demand of ourselves, the more it will be tested. Frankly, at times it would be easier in the short run to stuff issues away, but the dividends that have come back positively have made each choice worth all the perceived risk.

"L" for Loser

Have you ever seen the movie *Sandlot*? It is one of my (Brenda's) favorite movies. It's about some neighborhood kids playing baseball

back in the 1960s. There is one point where rival kids are interacting and the name calling starts. Someone calls the other a big "L.7. weenie" and puts the "L" for loser on his forehead (this symbol was further popularized by the song "You're an Allstar" by Smash Mouth). We were reminded of this concept when we attended a seminar by Ron Deal, "Building a Successful Stepfamily."[4]

> *Courage grows strength from a wound.*

Deal suggested that, especially in the church, if you have been divorced or remarried you sometimes feel like you have a big "D" for divorced or "R" for remarried on your forehead. Ron suggests that we change it up and consider the "D" to stand for delivered and the "R" to stand for redeemed. What a fresh concept in the midst of the shame that can sometimes accompany the journey of being divorced and remarried. It's a wonderful reminder that the ground is level at the foot of the cross.

Was what Jesus did on the cross good enough for my sin(s) involved in my divorce? Can we accept His forgiveness to truly be delivered and redeemed? God never moves out of our lives...we are the ones who move. It is our choice where we want the Lord to be in our lives.

Let's look at one more issue:

Prayer/Spiritual Dimension

We are certified to give the Prepare and Enrich[5] assessment. Prepare and Enrich (P and E) is part of Life Innovations, Inc., founded by renowned marriage researcher David Olson. Many clergy offer the assessment to couples as part of their marriage counseling. Questions

pertaining to communication, finances, leisure activities, and family of origin give couples a very balanced and thorough view of their relationship. We recommend doing this assessment, whether you are engaged or have been married fifty years. The assessment rates marriages in one of five levels: Devitalized, Conflicted, Traditional, Harmonious, and Vitalized. The goal is to have a vitalized marriage. The one difference between the Harmonious and Vitalized marriage levels is the spiritual component of prayer.

We don't want just a good marriage, we want a GREAT marriage. Having prayer in our marriage has made all the difference.

I (Gil) know as a man that prayer is very intimate between spouses, but it can be intimidating at the same time. We have talked to so many couples who do not pray together because it seems awkward or it is not clear who is expected to lead the prayer.

I find it hard to pray together when there is something between the two of us. The temptation to pray *at* each other instead of *for* each other can become apparent. Like, "Lord, make my wife desire to have sex with me more often," or "Lord, make my husband more understanding of my feelings and lose some weight while you've got his attention!"

We recently interviewed a marriage pastor about prayer in marriages. He shared that in the majority of marriages he had worked with, couples are not praying together and men are not leading spiritually. Why is that? Do men feel ill equipped or afraid of "What will my wife think?" Do they feel foolish? Guys, there are plenty of materials to arm you to be a spiritual leader in your home. One that I suggest is by Stu Weber in his book *The Heart of a Tender Warrior.*[6] Being a "manly man," especially in leading in the spiritual life of your marriage, really calls upon men to be brave and courageous! It does not take much bravery on your part if she is leading the way. As I reflect on this point, I am reminded of an old Latin saying:

> *"Courage grows strength from a wound."*

You may ask, what does that have to do with prayer? For me, I tried to lead in this area, but my first wife did not follow really well. To take the risk of trying again, I had to accept my wound and try to lead again.

This dimension of prayer was a choice I made from the get-go.

When Gil leads our marriage in this area, I (Brenda) find him even more attractive. Statistics show that couples who pray together have an incredible sexual relationship. So our recommendation is, please go pray.

It's the right thing to do.

Note to the Guys from Gil

If you are not praying together at this point, I encourage you to take the first step. When you go to bed at night, just thank the Lord for the day. If morning is better, ask Him to lead you through your day, together! Skills take time to perfect and muscles develop over time,

Guys, believe me, most women long for you to lead in this area of the marriage.

The very thing that seems to portray weakness becomes a strength the two of you can draw from. Wives with husbands who pray and guys who make room for their wives to pray openly enjoy an intimacy beyond those who don't.

Misleading Myths

Here are five interesting myths that many stepfamilies resonate with. How about you?

1. Putting unrelated people in the same house will bring them to love and care for one another.

    Believe it or not, love and care may OR may not develop. Developing love and care for someone is like intimacy. Intimacy develops over

a long period of time, it does not happen overnight. The key is to be patient and allow everyone to move at their own pace, not forcing intimacy. We need to keep in mind the big picture. You are totally committed to this family, you're not going anywhere, right? So whether it takes six months or forty years, you'll be there to support and encourage each member of the family right where they are at. We're not saying that this is always easy, but it's the right thing to do. When in doubt, just love on them.

2.   This marriage/family is competing against the legacy of the previous one.

This time there are different people involved, different dynamics. Don't get caught up in the "it used to be this way" mentality, which will just get you in trouble. DON'T COMPARE. Live in the present and accept your stepfamily for what it is. God calls us to be faithful with what stands directly in front of us. We cannot resurrect something that is dead. Do we really want to? Would that positively impact our current situation? Sometimes it feels easier to resort to old patterns even if they were unhealthy because they are familiar. Being uncomfortable can be a positive circumstance because this is an opportunity to try something new. A chance to rely on the Lord to work through you without having all the answers yourself! In the following chapters we'll give you a lot of tools to do this!

Put ourselves in our kid's shoes...

3.   Everything will fall into place.

We want this marriage to have everything in its place as soon as possible so we can all be happy…right? Then we can get on with life. Do you realize that the average stepfamily takes seven years to integrate according to E. Mavis Hetherington?[7] Wow! So when we talk with families that are a few months into their new family and things are a little rocky, this statistic brings in a welcomed reality check. We always hear a sigh of relief and renewed hope. Keep in mind that this is a general statistic in stepfamilies. We realize that some families will fall into place faster than others…and some may never achieve harmony.

4.   The kids will be happy about the remarriage.

Doesn't that just make sense? We were thrilled to find love again—a new start, new adventures. In reality, stepfamilies are born out of loss. The previous marriage may have ended due to the death of a spouse. Sometimes the ghost of memory of the deceased parent may come back and add strife for the new stepparent. The previous marriage may have ended due to divorce. Children still want their biological parents to remarry or have the deceased parent come back to life. Both situations have huge emotional consequences. One thing that we remind ourselves often is to put ourselves in our kids' shoes. Don't underestimate the positive and negative emotions you receive from your kids. They can both happen at the same time!

5.   You both learned from past mistakes and won't make them again.

Be open to revisiting past blunders even though you feel that you dealt with them. Make sure you haven't missed anything. Just because you feel you have dealt with it and "put it on the shelf" doesn't mean you can't pull it down to look at again. This is a new relationship now and may bring new light to old stuff.

The circumstances and attitudes of your previous actions or motives require a true change of heart. Don't sit there so long that you have a pity party or get totally stuck. Do business and move forward…always forward.

These are just a few common myths. There are lots more, we're sure. For us, just facing the reality of these false dictates has helped us adjust our expectations so that we can be more effective with our kids and more loving to each other.

Do you know why relationships fail? You might say adultery, addiction, or abuse, and those would be very good reasons. But one of the main reasons relationships fail is because of flat-out selfishness. We think: "It's more important for me to get what I want, the way I want it right now." All I know is when I (Brenda) serve my husband, an incredible thing happens. He serves me back! I don't ask him to, it just happens. We **both** serve each other. This is such a simple act that can absolutely revolutionize your marriage.

Just to clarify, this is not a contest to see who can out-serve each other. It might be as simple as bringing your spouse a cup of coffee in the morning. I think sometimes we treat our friends better than we treat our spouses. If you can't handle the word "serve" yet, try this: just be nice to each other. I'm sure you have heard your mom say, "A little bit of kindness can go a long way."

Do you want a GREAT marriage?

We are going to give you some incredible tools to use, but keep in mind this whole selfishness component. It can sneak in when you least expect it!

During our stepfamily adventure, over and over it is confirmed to us how important our marriage is. We DO NOT want our kids to experience another divorce. We want them to experience what a healthy marriage looks like. Our passion and focus is to keep our marriage strong, not only for the sake of our kids, but also for each other and the legacy of this new family. Through our time together in this book, you will be reminded of our byline:

If you ain't got the marriage, you ain't got nothin'.

End of Chapter Questions

At the end of each chapter you will find some questions. Some of these will be quite easy for you to answer. Others may take some time and gut-wrenching thought. Did we say this was going to be easy? Either way, we challenge you to take the time to answer these, first by yourself and then with your spouse. We know through doing this that your relationship will grow to a deeper level of understanding, therefore giving you strength as a couple. It's totally worth it, trust us! Have fun with the action items too!

1. Where are you with your relationship to God?
    Do you feel He: (circle all that apply)

    a. has abandoned you

    b. has given you wisdom

    c. was/is a trusted companion

    d. made you feel guilty

    e. has restored you, or...

    f. _____(fill in the blank)

2. On a scale of 1–10 (1 being low, 10 being high)

    Where are you at in the process of:

    Confession _____

    Redemption _____

    Repentance _____

3. On a scale of 1–10 (1 being low, 10 being high)

    How is our relationship doing with trust? _____

    How is our relationship doing with honesty? _____

4. Where/when was your trust and honesty violated in your life?

    _____

    _____

    _____

5. Have you experienced forgiveness from your divorce? Have you forgiven? At what level?

    _____

    _____

    _____

6. Do you feel safe in your relationship with your spouse? If not, how can he/she help you in that process?

    _____

    _____

    _____

7. What reactions have you had from people when they find out you're part of a stepfamily? (Do you hear "you're like the Brady Bunch" a lot?)

_____

_____

_____

8. What unrealistic expectations have you had with your remarriage and stepfamily?

_____

_____

_____

9. Have you been encouraged or discouraged by these expectations and why?

_____

_____

_____

Action Item

Go for a walk to get some fresh air (always holding hands!).

"The goal in marriage is not to think alike,

but to think together."

—Robert C. Dodds

Restored & Remarried

Chapter 2

The Wall

Chapter 2

The Wall

One of the biggest misconceptions about remarriage is that we can treat it like our first marriage. We have talked with well meaning pastors (whom we have the utmost respect for) who counsel remarriages and stepfamilies and offer advice as if these were first marriages. This can be damaging. We were at a stepfamily conference years ago and there was a pastor sitting in one of the workshops. As the presenter unwrapped the diversities of a stepfamily, this pastor soon realized that he had been offering bad counsel. Not intentionally, but he just didn't understand the real challenges stepfamilies have. He thought marriage was marriage and remarriage issues were no different.

Take discipline for example. The man is the man of his house, right? He needs to keep order and lay down the law and keep all the kids in line. In a newly forming stepfamily this can be devastating. Everyone is still adjusting, especially the kids. Discipline takes time, and respect

is to be earned by the stepparent. This does not happen overnight and especially not in a heavy-handed manner. This pastor was thankful to gather information to understand the animal of stepfamily life. Even those of us in stepfamilies should be in constant learning mode to stay ahead of any relational disasters that may be around the next corner with kids, spouses, in-laws, ex-laws, and the family pet!

When we meet with couples who are contemplating remarriage we make it tough on them. We help them take off the rose-colored glasses to see what they are really getting into. What are they made of? What will they do when the ex is manipulative or disrespectful? How will they handle teens in the home when their hormones kick in? And what about old memories or patterns that are destructive to the new relationship? (We offer positive solutions to this challenge in the coming pages!) Where is your level of commitment to the marriage? Hard-hitting questions, but we would rather have that couple not marry if it means saving them and their kids from another divorce!

So, there are usually two ways people think about remarriage. The first is to treat it like a first marriage. For those of you who are already remarried, you already understand the differences. Things that may have worked the first time around aren't working this time.

> *We get the adventure,*
> *God gets the glory!*

And the second way to think about remarriage is, "Hey, this is tough stuff. Let's bag it and run," or "Boy, this is not what I wanted." "There are too many issues to have to deal with." "I don't want to have to contend with 'my stuff.' I may be exposed."

There's a third choice. Is it possible to have joy and fulfillment in a

remarriage? Isn't that the point of getting married again? Why would we want to be in a relationship full of bitterness and misunderstandings… maybe again? You have to be in adventure mode to remarry again! There are many blessings that come with the adventure. Bottom line thoughts:

- Yeah, this is tough. So what? I'm up for it. Bring it on!

- It's not all honeymoon stage. (*Do you realize that remarried people usually have their honeymoon after the kids move out?*)

- I am in this for the long haul.

- Commitment with a capital "C." I am not afraid of it.

- No "back door" of the "D" word (divorce) in our vocabulary. This is not even an option (short of abuse).

The adventure of a healthy remarriage can be full of incredible blessings. It may test you at times, but if you are willing to work through the challenges and keep the above list in mind, you will be a better person for it and have a stronger marriage. And what better gift can you give your children (and friends) than modeling a healthy, happy marriage, even if it is the second time around?

From early on in our relationship our motto has always been:

We get the adventure, God gets the glory!

ROI in Your Marriage and Family

ROI is short for "Return on Investment." It is a term usually found in the business world. An investor expects a positive return on his money or assets when put into a venture or the stock market. Now those who lost millions during the stock market crash of 2008 would say that this principle can backfire. My reply would be, "Yes it can." In the sense of money markets and the unfortunate practice of dishonesty or trickery for gain, you can lose big time. But the principle as a whole still stands true, for often in business or relationships you get out of them what you put in.

In much the same way, ROI applies to your family life. Making deposits of love, respect, honesty, commitment, and trust affords each person to also make withdrawals when needed. The key is not to cause an overdraft on your account.

I've heard it said that loving someone is having a ready attitude to do kind things for one another. That means you should be looking for ways to serve and show that you cherish them. That includes acts or words that touch them personally. When this becomes habit, the principle of ROI often diminishes selfishness and keeps the couple balanced.

Investing in your marriage and family will decrease the myths that we mentioned earlier.

Here are a few examples or outcomes with the best possible ROI's:

- Your new marriage can be mutually satisfying, both emotionally and physically.

- Healthy marriages modeled for children restore well-being for children.

- Stepfamily members have the opportunity to learn from their mistakes, offer forgiveness to one another, and heal the pain from the past.

- Living in a stepfamily, we all learn about diversity and differences, adaptability and flexibility, which in turn will empower our kids as they deal with the real world and its challenges—therefore making them stronger, healthier adults.

Children who have lived through the experience of a previous bad marriage can be positively influenced when living in a home where a good marriage is modeled. With an ROI attitude the new couple has a great opportunity to affect future generations.

To get a great, positive, ROI type experience for both you and your kids, the best thing you can do is strengthen the marriage. It is priority number one! Again, do not underestimate the power of prayer through

this stepfamily adventure! We pray for wisdom constantly, not to mention sanity and the need for a sense of humor!

Much like the stock market crash of 2008, there were adversities in our first marriages that contributed to failure and dismal results. So to think that remarriage will not have challenges in similar fashion, one would be living on another planet. Remarriage is tough. And all of you who are reading this know that first marriages crumble even when you think you are doing all the right stuff. But remarriage has challenges that first-time marriages don't encounter.

Think about it. What things can come against your remarriage that are different from the first time around? For instance, the kids may not be yours but are from another marriage or relationship. How are you going to handle that? Add to it the complexity of children you may have from your previous marriage and you have quite the recipe for craziness.

> *To get a great, positive, ROI type experience, strengthen the marriage.*

Clearly, you now have an ex-spouse! That alone is a new twist. Due to death or divorce, that person has an affect upon your new marriage! Whether the old spouse lives across town or in another state, they are part of your personal life journey. If you are a widower or widow, the "ghost" of your former spouse can have an effect from the grave as well. What do you do with that?

Are you beginning to see the picture?

How about money and finances? You may have heard that this issue is in the top two reasons for arguments and divorce. (The other one that made the top two is communication.) Money is tough, and with it come several challenges. Who did the checkbook before—you or the ex? Who is going to handle the finances in the new marriage? Talk about adversity! If this issue does not get settled early on, your crash could look much like Wall Street at its worst.

Health issues also can add new stress. Whether it be you, your new spouse, or one of your children, it is all part of the package. How will these new challenges affect your attitude and love for your new mate? Life is hard. Is love enough?

Wait! We're not done yet! Think for a moment regarding your schedules and traditions, just to name a couple more challenges. Sure, we all face these facts of life and day-to-day tasks; you may say: "What is the big deal?" Just for a moment take off the blinders and see that if these factors were reasons for your first marriage to have conflict, how much more will they impact a remarriage? If you were unable to keep it together in that relationship, what is different this time?

Not to be naïve, but did you realize that our society and western culture is attacking our marriages and families on a regular basis? Healthy marriages and families are the backbone of our God-fearing country. To indulge a step further, would we be totally ignorant not to think or consider that we have a spiritual enemy who wants to distract, discourage, and defeat us? If you don't believe me, just read 1 Peter 5:8.

Respectfully we'd like to shout a warning to remarried couples. BEWARE OF BECOMING ISOLATED! A couple can easily self-destruct without the encouragement and support of others. They need individuals willing to offer perspective along with second opinions where situations appear impossible. In terms of military conflict, if a solider or troop can be isolated, they are easier to pick off and defeat. Similarly, remarried couples left feeling alone can begin to experience failure, and the memory of "oh no, not again" sets in. Those who have support have a fighting chance to come out stronger, not defeated.

One critical tool you need to know for success is the 60/80 Rule. Let's unpack the concept for you by the numbers as it is statistically backed. 60 percent of second marriages fail within the first two years. That

result is due to a variety of issues, with the kids as the top factor. But the good news is that 80 percent of that population could have avoided another divorce given two factors being part of their new marriage.[1]

1. Information & Resources

2. Support & Encouragement

Our point here is that even healthy relationships will face turmoil. The key is what skills and support do you have to keep your relationship healthy and vibrant amidst the grind of life?

Isn't love enough? Oh, marriage will be different this time around! Really?

How are you going to protect your marriage?

The Wall

We'd like to share a concept with you that has strengthened our marriage and continues to develop. It's called "The Wall." Usually walls are barriers or obstacles that are built in relationships to keep others out. These walls cannot be seen, but they are there keeping things at bay. Trying to get through or around them to reach another person can take an epic effort.

We turned the perception of walls into a positive concept. It was part of our own restoration process. Our wall was not to separate us. Instead, our wall was one we could BOTH get behind to continue to be restored and have a safe place to protect our marriage. It was a buffer to allow us as a couple to come together, regroup, rest, and, yes, hide from incoming attacks.

Example: We had a full weekend planned with kid activities. The ex threw a wrench into our plans that affected all kids involved. It was easy to have the stress come between us. "They're not even my ex, and now it is impacting how I get to interact with my kids this weekend." We went so far as to build a wall out of old play bricks. Here is how the story unfolded...

RESTORED &
Remarried

I (Gil) was reading from the book of Nehemiah in the Old Testament of the Bible. In chapter 4 Nehemiah has returned to Jerusalem to find the walls broken down, cracked, burned, and in ruins. The people were devastated. The great city could no longer serve as the fortress it once was. They felt, and were, defenseless. Honestly, I felt the same way when I got started into this new marriage. It was not only remarriage, it was rebuilding our lives out of the ruins of divorce.

The safety we knew and experienced in our first marriages was gone. The walls that had been built to seemingly protect us and our family had crashed. The family that had worked and played together had been scattered. Now the task to start fresh and bring it all back together again appeared less likely than ever before. Being aware that that hurt and distrust was under the surface was uncomfortable to say the least. My kids and Brenda's kids and all the brokenness of life were the building blocks handed to us.

As I (Gil) read and prayed about the common thread, a revelation was given. In Nehemiah, God gave the people the heart to build and shore up the walls for their own protection. As I shared this with Brenda she recalled some old play building brick blocks under the bed of one of her boys (my new son). I went upstairs and dug around until I found the blocks. Once I finally found them, I was amazed. The irony was dripping from the story. As I pulled out each one of these toy blocks—each one the size of real bricks—I noticed their condition. Like any toy a young boy might play with, the bricks were smashed, torn, had holes punched in them, and were pretty well beat up. They were perfect! For demonstration purposes we physically built a wall out of these bricks that we share at our seminar.

Nehemiah used the beat up stones and bricks of Jerusalem's ruins to rebuild the city. In the same way, we felt like we were being handed the same challenge. Our lives were bruised and tattered. But by God's grace He would take the ruins and rebuild, as long as we would have a heart to work and build the wall for our protection.

The key cornerstones we placed at the foundation were Christ and Commitment. Since these principles had been damaged so severely at the end of our first marriages, we vowed to have them firmly in place at the beginning of our new marriage to build the rest of our wall.

Answering my (Gil) own question, "How are you going to protect your marriage?" puts this concept to the test often. There are many circumstances that get thrown at us as individuals and as a couple that destroy trust and safety in the relationship. Choosing to get behind the wall that we build and maintain is just that, a choice.

Kids, ex's, and finances are just a few examples that can be like bombshells blasting against your wall. What is your plan? We suggest building your wall so when those times come, you can stand behind the wall for protection rather than division. Be prepared, because kid issues can be some of the biggest bombshells.

How did we handle the ex wrenched weekend? It would have been easy to become defensive or accusatory of the ex. We had to refocus our attention on getting behind our wall. With creative solutions we were able to accommodate each individual that was affected. The wall acted as a buffer between us and the circumstances. Flexibility was key.

Building Blocks

Psalm 118:22 reads:

> *"The stone which the builders rejected has become the chief cornerstone."*

Christ is referenced as the chief cornerstone. The understanding of Christ's position, the rejected stone, gave fuller meaning to placing Christ at the center of our life and marriage. The foundation of our marriage has to be Jesus Christ.

Ephesians 5:25 states how Christ loved the church and gave of Himself to establish relationship with us. His initiation of loving us as His bride is an apt example. In other words, Christ pursued us first. He chose to illustrate His model via the relationship of a husband to his wife.

We knew of this principle, but had to consciously put it into place! Husbands, love your wives as Christ loves the church. Gentlemen, that is a tall order to say the least! Once a right relationship between man and wife is established, the foundation is set for building in all the other

principles that make a solid marriage. Christ is the example. Follow His lead, men, and then women can trust Him in you to follow willingly in the role for which they were designed.

Christ is a sure foundation not only in marriage but also for your life. Whether a person chooses to adopt that belief is their choice. I (Gil) have a friend who is on marriage number three. The first two marriages were self-centered and ended with a lot of heartache. This guy had a lot of work to do internally and he chose to face the pain. He took the long road and process of healing of his character faults to be prepared for his current marriage. He confessed to me that Christ is now the focal point and this marriage is on far more solid ground.

> ## *You don't want a good marriage...*

You may recall the statistics we brought up earlier about Prepare and Enrich, where the vitalized vs. harmonious marriages have a deeper (spiritual) component. I'm sure my friend would testify to the truth of this study. He has challenges with stepkids and his own kids, but the enjoyment of the current marriage is far more satisfying than he had known before.

Two more building blocks to include in your wall are pivotal and are just as important as the foundational blocks I've described thus far. They are trust and honesty. More than likely, trust and honesty were eroded in your last relationship. With that, you are more likely to protect your heart and hide true feelings. And that's where the difficulty comes.

Honesty is like emotional nudity. It is your true self unedited, yet tempered. And along with that comes trust, which knows you are loved no matter what you share. With trust, you know you have a place to

be vulnerable even if you feel you are exposing yourself. Mysteriously, the two go hand in hand. You can't have one without the other. When the two characteristics of trust and honesty are in harmony, the protection of the wall just increased its strength and satisfaction level 100 percent.

Building your wall is an ongoing process. Keeping the bricks in good shape and connected is what is going to help your wall last for the long haul. When you look at brickwork, what is holding the bricks together? Mortar.

In our analogy of the wall, our mortar is safety. Safety is what holds your relationship together so that you can share trust and honesty with each other. And interestingly, there are many parallels between mortar and safety:

- The strength of your masonry work depends largely on the mortar you use. *The safety factor of your wall will bring your wall strength.*

- To mix mortar, you use a ratio of three parts masonry sand (builders sand, if it is very clean) to one part masonry cement. *To make safety mortar use three parts pliable heart and one part grace. I know this is corny, but work with me (Brenda)!*

- Add water to the dry materials and mix to a consistency like pudding. Too dry, and it will be difficult to "set" the brick in the mortar bed; too wet, and the brick will sag. *Make sure you are real with each other. If you're not, your wall won't be worth anything and won't be able to stand the forces that will come against it. Don't be a poser!*

- Space mortar boards (what the mortar is mixed on) about every six feet along the wall or on each side if the project is small. This will allow you to grab mortar with your trowel as you work, and not have to move around too much. *As you create your wall, have those safety spaces close by as you come upon uncomfortable situations. You won't waste as much time emotionally.*

- At all times the mortar should be kept well-tempered, that is, of the proper working consistency. And the board should be kept well-supplied at all times. Some contractors find it economical to hire a mortar tender to keep the mortar tempered. *The safety of your relationship should be a healthy place that has a comfortable consistency for both of you. Invite your mortar tender to be Jesus Christ.*

How would you gauge safety in your previous marriage/relationship? Could you share anything you felt needed to be said? Or was the information used against you and not held in confidence? Were you supported? Do you feel like you were heard?

Ladies, let me (Brenda) address you for a moment on this issue of safety. When it comes to sharing delicate issues, most women have a higher level of safety than men. How many times do we share deep secrets with our girlfriends? Usually we are supportive of one another and give encouraging words, or at least have an attentive ear. We may laugh together and even shed a tear or two. It's like a mini-estrogen fest!

How often do you give your man a place to do that? (Not that he wants to be at an estrogen fest.) If your man has the courage to share what he is really feeling, do you listen or do you blow him off? Do you keep eye contact and let him speak at his own pace without interrupting? Do you affirm him as your provider, protector, and warrior? He is a warrior, you know. Even though he may not be doing what you think he should be doing, are you his biggest cheerleader? It can be really intimidating for men to share, especially if they have been laughed at, ridiculed, or emasculated in the past.

Men learn lessons quickly. It only takes once or twice for a guy to be shut down and they won't go down that path again. As wives, it should be our honor and privilege for our man to share with us. We need to be a safe place for him, not only for the sake of our wall but also for the legacy of our new family. Safety keeps the bricks secure. It makes the wall solid. It allows us to withstand the storms of life, because there will be storms.

Of course, there are relationships where the guy may feel it safe to share. Guys, everything I said to the ladies applies to you as well. I challenge you to think through how safe you are making your marriage. Does your wife feel safe to share what is on her heart? Do you honestly listen, or do you shut her down? Are you letting her know that she is cherished and that she makes you feel like a man? Do you let her know that she is a "wanted woman" and not just in the bedroom? Does she know that you are battling for her heart? The bigger question is…are you?

We'd like to share with you a list from the following profound little book, *Lists to Live by for Every Married Couple.*[2] It was compiled by Dr. Steve Stephens, Alice Gray, and John Van Diest. The suggested actions and attitudes will build your wall or bust your wall! Getting trust and honesty right will allow you to build confidently. If, for any reason, you feel a lack of safety is a factor, stop what you are doing and make the corrections immediately! Ask for forgiveness if it's your issue or be kind and seek understanding if it is your spouse. Make sure you are both building with clean mortar.

If you want a different result in this area of your marriage, you have to do things a new way. Practicing the same old methods or habits brings no contentment. It will only make you go insane. So give these trust builders a try. These no brainers have surprising results.

Trust Builders:

1. Show others how proud you are of your spouse.

2. Keep your word.

3. Make your spouse a priority.

4. Know when your spouse is stressed and do what you can to reduce it.

5. Be dependable.

6. Never forget your anniversary.

7. Give each other space when needed and closeness the rest of the time.

8. Always wear your wedding ring.

Trust Busters:

1. Keep secrets from each other.

2. Not being honest.

3. Flirt with someone else.

4. Embarrass your spouse.

5. Break a promise.

6. Be critical.

7. Lack of follow-through.

8. Don't show complete, unselfish, committed love.

Walls have many bricks. As you read on you will find plenty of suggestions to add to your wall. But, like any relationship, your marriage has nuances of its own. For that, we've created something that will help you create your own unique bricks.

Your Brick and Mortar

Acrostics (when a set of letters from a number of words are used to create one specific word) are used in a variety of ways. They can be learning tools or used as memory triggers. And they can be very thought provoking.

Early on in our relationship we used acrostics to share and probe one another's hearts by key words. We would come up with different words to bring clarity to our relationship. And even now, many years later, we continue the process. It has gotten a little wacky and makes us laugh at times, but it has also added a depth to our marriage.

For example, we don't want a good marriage we want a GREAT marriage. What does a great marriage look like to us? We took the word GREAT and made it an acrostic. The words represented in the acrostic remind us of what we think great really is.

Example: GREAT

	Brenda	**Gil**
G	gentle/gain	godly focused
R	reality (don't lose touch with it)	restoration/restored hope
E	extravagant/eyes for you	excellence of spirit
A	anew (in a different or new form)	anticipate joint plans
T	testify (to what God is doing)	trust/treasure

Side note from Brenda: Gil had thousands of words more than me in his daily word list so I sometimes got some "encouragement" from the dictionary to stimulate my creative juices to find just the right word for my acrostic.

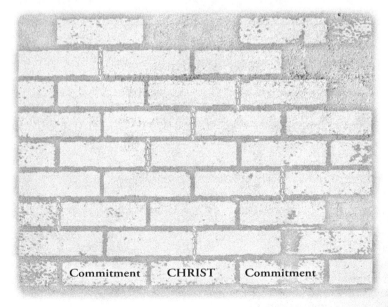

As you identify what words are important to you, add them as a new brick to your wall (please see chart on previous page).

New words equal new bricks. Create your own language. Create history for your marriage. It's fun to pick a word and work on it separately for a week or so. Then come back together and share what words you've come up with. This is great date material and you don't have to break the date rules. Oh, we haven't told you your date rules yet?

When you are on a date you cannot talk about money, kids, in-laws, ex-laws, the bills, schedules, house or car maintenance…need I go on? The most important thing you can do with each other is laugh. (Plus, it burns calories!)

End of Chapter Questions

1. What positive ROIs (Return on Investments) have you made in your marriage? What positive ROIs have you made in your stepfamily?

   _____

   _____

   _____

2. How have you been feeling isolated? What steps can you take to change the situation? Who can you talk to?

   _____

   _____

   _____

3. What's the condition of your mortar (safety): too hard and dry, too watery and wet, or just right?

_____

_____

_____

4. What are some of the adversities that bash/crash against your wall?

_____

_____

_____

5. Share a time when a wall was between you. Share a time when you felt you were both behind your wall and fought for the protection of your marriage.

_____

_____

_____

6. Safety in your marriage? Do you have more Trust Busters or Trust Builders?

_____

_____

_____

7. Create a GREAT acrostic for your marriage! Filling in your blocks in your wall is a process, it takes time. But talk about what building blocks you see as important now.

_____

_____

_____

Action Item:

Go on a date and share your acrostic and any new words you can work on. How is your wall evolving?

"Chains do not hold a marriage together.
It is threads, hundreds of tiny threads which sew
people together through the years.
That is what makes a marriage last—
more than passion or even sex!"

—Simone Signoret

RESTORED & Remarried

Chapter 3

"I Didn't Think It Was Going to Be Like This"

Chapter 3

"I Didn't Think It Was Going to Be Like This"

As Ashley sipped on her coffee she shared through her tears, "Everything seemed to be in place when we were dating and leading up to the wedding. Once we got married everything changed! The kids, who were all excited before the wedding, were now vying for their place in the family in negative ways. My husband keeps going over to his ex's to help her and I am finding that my old insecurities are starting to get in the way. I thought we'd be all one happy family. I didn't think it was going to be like this."

The first year of marriage will set the tone for your future. And for those first twelve months, if problems go unresolved they will come back to haunt you. Some very close friends of ours had been married for thirty-five years. They are just coming to the end of the process of their great train wreck (divorce). If that's not sad enough in itself, what's even worse is that they are both complaining about things that happened in their first year of marriage, thirty-five years ago! Wow, how many layers of hurts and unresolved issues were piled on top of that first year stuff? If only they had the skills, the courage, or maybe the safety to deal with those issues head on, they wouldn't be in the situation they are in today.

> *The first year of marriage will set the tone for your future.*

David Olson, founder of Life Innovations and the Prepare and Enrich Inventory, has interviewed hundreds of thousands of people about their marriage. He found that 53 percent of remarried people have not worked through their past hurts. Are you part of that 53 percent? I have found that sometimes I (Brenda) think I have worked through all my hurts and then something will come up to remind me that I need to look at it all again, going deeper, digging through layers. I think of hurt as an onion. As I cut through the first layers my eyes begin tearing up. I may stop to wipe them and need to take a break because the aroma is so strong. But the sooner I can cut all the way through and get to the core, the better. Depending on where we are in life, we may only be able to handle our hurts one layer at a time. And there will be tears. But ultimately we need to get to the core. And no matter how long it takes or how hard it gets, that is our job if we want to see our marriage succeed. We must figure out what the underlying issue is that is causing the pain. Is it abuse, abandonment, addiction, or unrealistic expectations?

This is part of the fine-tuning process the Lord uses in order to make us more like Him. This peeling away can only happen when we trust Him to do the work in us. We must surrender to Him and the process.

RESTORED &
Remarried

I love to quote my husband here because he is living proof of this: "The cure for the pain is in the pain; run to it, not from it." Is this an easy thing to do? Absolutely not. But it's a quicker, more thorough route to healing. Life is hard enough. The sooner we can heal from some of our hurts, the lighter our load will be and the freer we will be to love our life and those around us.

Another survey that Life Innovations did was to ask remarried couples what their top two factors were for marital satisfaction. Any guesses as to what they are? You probably guessed the first—communication. When good communication is happening in a marriage, you can conquer the world! Do you know the second? Leisure time. I (Brenda) know I underestimate the fun factor in our relationship. I get so busy with what's going on in the day-to-day demands that I have to do a self-check to see if we're having enough fun. This may come easier for some of you. But for me I have to make an intentional effort to go out of my routine to get a little crazy. Gil and I often say "we're not laughing enough," and then we go do something we enjoy!

Activities that we enjoy can be as simple as a hike up Mount Hamilton in the Columbia River Gorge or a fine cup of coffee at Starbucks on Northwest 23rd in Portland. The relationship is to be fun and enjoyed. Often it's pretty easy, but when times get rocky we put into practice a course of action that settles us and gets us back on the right path.

Are you part of that 53 percent?

Love Triangle

You may have seen the Love Triangle before, yet it is worthwhile to refresh your memory. When overwhelmed, our ability to be charitable, fun-loving, or patient can be diminished. To "get yourself right," your walk with God comes first, then your walk with your mate. In the illustration on the next page there is a visual of what is happening:

The closer we draw to God as individuals the more intimate we become to God, "righting ourself," so to speak. At the same time the marriage relationship between wife and husband becomes closer. As you move toward Christ, the focus is an interdependent relationship, rather than a dependent relationship. Knowing that Brenda is a wonderful woman and I'm (Gil) a pretty cool guy is not enough to rely on in the relationship.

Our marriage is stronger because of the balance of our Love Triangle. This triangle also strengthens our wall. You may feel at times that it is a fight to protect your wall. You're right. It's a battle. It's a battle for the hearts of each other and our kids. The battle is to keep everyone in an emotionally healthy place so they can be their best. Don't let "things" come between you and your wall, especially the kids! This is a tough balancing act. We're not putting the marriage before the kids; it's the foundation FOR the kids.

In the foundation of your wall, Jesus Christ is the cornerstone. We've already talked about that. Well, the cornerstone of your Love Triangle is also Christ. Conceptually, the triangle is important to any marriage

relationship—all the more important to remarriage. As we've stated previously, marriage principles of any kind do apply to remarriage, but there are still differences between the two.

When a person accepts his/her worth from God because of what Jesus did on the cross, they realize it cannot be earned. It is a gift. You are not dependent on your family for your sense of self-worth, but on your God. We can't get caught up in getting our self-worth from our spouse, either. And, in the same breathe, our self-worth cannot be taken away by our stepchildren. This can be hard if your relationship with them is strained or manipulative tactics are going on.

If we reach out to our stepkids and try to be positive and nurturing and we don't receive that back, we can take that as a personal blow to who we are. Consider the source of where their negative attitudes are coming from. They are working out of pain and confusion a lot of the time. (We'll talk more about this in Chapter 5.)

Just be reminded that you have a heavenly Father who gave His life for you and knows every inch of your heart. He wants you to succeed in your stepfamily. He is there to carry you through the tough times and rejoice with you in the good times. When we recognize and accept these truths about the Lord, it strengthens our relationship with our spouse. When my (Brenda) relationship with the Lord is growing and deepening, my relationship with Gil does the same. This affects our kids too.

Run to it, not from it.

Speaking of Kids…

Speaking of our kids, there are some unique characteristics for remarriage concerning the kids. Marriage in general (even the first time) can be vulnerable to the kids. The demands that they place on

a marriage, intentionally or not, can be overwhelming at times. We're talking about schedules, rules, homework, their social connections, computer time, and of course their activities—be it dance or football. Even if your children are out of the house, there are dynamics that can affect your relationship. If the attitude of the marriage is survival mode or denial that anything is wrong, it is very easy to hide behind the kids and their activities.

In the name of being a good parent, many of us fall into this routine. What happens to the marriage in the meantime? Distance between the couple becomes greater, communication lessens, and your mortar (safety) in your wall starts chipping away. Typically, second marriages break up over the children. Once again, speaking out of both sides of our mouth, love on your kids (and your stepkids) but don't forget about the marriage. Remember:

If you ain't got the marriage, you ain't got nothin'.

Loyalty issues were the topic of a talk show hosted by Dr. Laura one day. She received a phone call from a stepparent who was having huge problems with the kids coming between the husband and wife. The circumstances were classic in that each biological parent would side with their children rather than the spouse to have a united front on issues. The old "divide and conquer" routine…it was tearing the couple apart!

Dr. Laura's reply was "accept and deal with it because the parent/child bond won't change and kids will wedge between the married couple. In stepfamilies that is just the way it is."

Get behind your wall!

By the time she got to that comment, I (Gil) had wandered closer to the radio that was in my office. Being so passionate about what she was

saying, I became irritated with her lack of counsel to the caller to share with them some hope or instruction to fight for their marriage first. I blurted out loud in the middle of my office forgetting who would hear...

"IT CAN CHANGE IF YOU ARE COMMITTED TO THE MARRIAGE AND EACH OTHER!"

Get behind your wall!

After realizing two co-workers were staring at me, I cooled off and went back to my desk. Family life is built on the marriage, I concluded, especially in a remarriage. It became very clear at that moment that most problems kids and families face have their roots in a weak marriage.

Depending on what your previous marriage was like, this is a chance to model a strong family foundation for your kids to carry on in their lives. As a father of seven (four of my own and three stepkids), the tactics kids take to manipulate the parents can be dicey territory. This is old news to most parents about how our kids attempt to play us.

When it is your own child, there is love and tolerance given as you teach and guide them from a young age. But if it happens to be a stepchild (who is ten and you think they should know better), let's say these temperaments can tend to tick you off. Your patience is not half as long.

If the concept of the wall is not understood or utilized, the couple may complain or, worst yet, lash out against each other, disrupting the marriage. The kids win—or seem to. Now, I must ask myself and you the reader, do the kids really win in the long haul when they are allowed to create issues between you and your spouse? We have come full circle where a choice must be made.

Will you have an attitude of commitment that keeps you investing in your marriage first? Don't get me wrong here, the kids have suffered. I know that. Really, I know that. But why did all that pain have to be endured by everyone? The marriage failed plain and simple. The kids and stepkids have their place, but the marriage is the bedrock to hold everything in place.

RESTORED &
Remarried

Commitment

After doing a lot of reading about this issue, we came across two quotes that are worthy to share with you:

"True commitment means much more than simply committing to staying married. Genuine commitment involves being committed to the growth and best interest of your partner."

—Jeff Herring, Oregonian Newspaper (2004)

"OK, you're committed to your marriage. Are you committed to being unhappy and miserable or are you committed to change?"[1]

—Autumn Ray, Marriage Team

Strengthening and protecting the commitment in our marriage and stepfamily life, we knew that good communication would be essential. So that you are on the same page and the relationship can flourish, trust and honesty must grow. Working on building and maintaining your wall is foundational.

We found materials that helped, like *Saving Your Second Marriage Before It Starts*[2] by Drs. Les and Leslie Parrot; *God Breathes on Blended Families*[3] by Moe and Paige Becnel; and *The Smart Stepfamily*[4] by Ron Deal. For more detail on these books please refer to the Stepfamily Resources section at the back.

As good as these materials were, they just did not give us the terms we were looking for and had begun to build for ourselves. For instance, have you ever had a situation related to your remarriage and stepfamily that you just can't find words to describe?

As a response, we created a practical tool. It was a way to express what was going on inside as we encountered the new marriage, stepkids, financial stresses, and even sexual issues. Sharing these terms with you is rather personal as it's a language of our own. Each term grew out of our past experiences where we had to be honest with ourselves and each other. As an act of trust, we peeled back the layers of who we were and how the past affected the present. The requirement for safety and to fight for each other's hearts was real stuff. Prayer was key as we faced each painful encounter together. To reassure our hearts, often we would turn to each other and state, "I am not going anywhere."

Personally, I (Gil) could not have put this into practice and lead, had I not done some internal work on my own. The works of John Eldredge, *The Sacred Romance*[5] and *Wild at Heart*,[6] were foundational to pointing me to principles of my walk with Jesus Christ. The use of modern authors and movies was also a reintroduction to my heart.

While we unpack these terms and techniques, I'd like you to think through what "catch" words you may have. The goal is to create **your** own language. Keep in mind your wall and who and what comes against it daily.

> *I am not going anywhere.*

Open Doors

The first term we'd like to share is called "Open Doors." Think of it this way:

Mental connection to the past. "Open Doors" are in direct correlation to "closed doors" of the true you and the real issues behind the authentic man or woman. In reading many of the authors mentioned earlier, self-talk is one discussion that never stops. Talking to yourself is OK. According to the experts, we all do it. But it's the answers to yourself that can get you into a heaping mess.

Remember, 53 percent of people are not dealing with their past hurts.

You need to learn to open up the real you. You need to find those past experiences in which you truly felt yourself. When were you not hiding behind the façade? When did you feel the most free? Explore your past. Try to learn from each memory—good or bad.

Think of it this way. Let's say there is a situation from your past that is very difficult to talk about. It could be about your childhood, parents, your kids, health, or previous relationships. The issue is locked up inside of you so, consequently, you are in lockdown. This closes a part of you off, not allowing true healthy intimacy to grow with your spouse. You get defensive and you can't or won't express your true feelings. There

*I realize it is my stuff...
the Cabo experience...*

is an emotional, mental gorilla behind one specific memory and it is affecting your entire life!

You may be afraid to bring up certain issues for a variety of reasons: jealousy, resentment, bitterness, insecurities, shame, or you may truly **believe** it is better left alone. You may feel a nudging from way down in your gut (most likely an urging from the Lord) that you really need

to share this with your spouse. But sadly, it's easier to bury it and not bring it up. A tug of war continues to motivate you to bury the matter. You conclude that, "It still hurts! I don't feel safe to share. Why rock the boat? This feeling to share will pass and I can patronize this gorilla another day. I'll look stupid (*I need to keep up my 'I got it together' look*)." You are uncertain of how to put it into words, so you let it go.

Am I the only one who has had the above conversation? This is just a thought, but maybe it's not you putting those thoughts into your head. Maybe a real battle is waging within you—a battle for your spiritual and emotional freedom. It's just a thought! Pray about it. Really!

Standing in front of a closed door, you shake inside with fear. You know what lies behind could be very difficult to face. Push through! To experience authentic transparency, you must open the door—at least to your spouse—to enjoy the intimacy you long for.

Men, this open door stuff was established early on when I (Gil) began to date Brenda. For women, the process is easier as they tend to share their feelings and have an abundance of words to get their stuff on the table. As guys, many of us work best in illustrations and concepts rather than feelings. So the term "Open Doors" was born! I employed it often and even to this day the major door that had to be opened occurred on our honeymoon. Talk about not thinking it would be this way…but I went for it. Here is the story and try not to laugh or cry. I'm a sensitive guy:

So, we finally made it to Cabo San Lucas, Mexico, for our honeymoon. My new bride was gorgeous, of course, and we were thoroughly enjoying ourselves—sleeping in, staying up late, and all that fun stuff! We rode horses on the beach, took excursions to watch whales—truly a perfect experience. Three days into it, as we are finishing up lunch on the balcony of our room overlooking the Sea of Cortez, I get hit with an issue. Out of the blue it brings me to a screeching halt. I go silent. Immediately I say to myself, "Stuff it. This isn't the place." But of course, I know that would be a bad move.

I think to myself: Well we are thirty miles to the airport. Catching a taxi or bus is not likely if she decides to bolt. And of course, I've been practicing trust and honesty the whole way so I can't flake out now on

our honeymoon, at the beginning of our new marriage. "So," I said to myself, "what are you going to do, superman?" The risk was huge!

"Brenda, come sit with me here in our room, I have something to share with you," I began. The look on her face was clear. She knew something was up and how she could read me was already recognized. Continuing into the confession that lay before me, she later shared that she felt safe. She wasn't concerned about what dark secret had

Is this a listen to listen or a listen to fix it?

not been revealed during the courtship and pre-marriage counseling. (Believe me, she did her homework on me!)

Often, when I had opened a door before, there was a pattern. I would look at the ceiling or sky and confide in the Father openly, much like the crazy Irishman who happened to be king of Ireland in the movie "Braveheart." "Well," I continued, "I have an Open Door to share with you and it is a disclosure that I feel has been brought to my attention with the worst timing ever. But I have to get it out in the open."

I stuttered and hemmed and hawed to get it out. She was patient. I finally was able to put the words together and I said, "This issue was a huge hindrance for me before in my ability to be at rest and intimate with complete confidence. It is not drugs or pornography or some external vice. It is *suspicion of you not being faithful.* I have struggled with this monster for years. Some of my suspicions were founded and others were not. And it was a weakness that caused a lot of havoc in my past!"

It was self talk that had gone bad. But I had determined that I would not take this "self talk discussion" into my new marriage! So there—

the monkey was off my back and in the middle of the room. I had been vulnerable and I felt exposed. But what was so cool about this episode of our honeymoon and new marriage is that often we reflect back to this specific Open Door. When I battle with suspicion now I realize it is my stuff and we handle it together, rather than allowing it to cause damage or distance. Now there is a term assigned to that door and I can call it the Cabo experience and she knows immediately right where I am. No matter what caused it, the issue is not something she did wrong but a battle she knows I fight, and now she can fight it with me.

I (Brenda) had to really understand the depth of what the Cabo experience meant to Gil. A few times after he identified that he felt this way, I would find myself feeling like, "Here we go again. Why is he thinking like this? Haven't I done everything I know to have him trust me and feel secure in our relationship?" It would be very easy to let myself get resentful and defensive. But I always reminded myself of the intensity of what the Cabo experience meant. We were still building history with each other and that takes time.

This experience taught me (Gil) that once a closed door is opened and the issue is exposed with safety in place, the very thing that is choking you will be disarmed. In this case a mental hang-up was a weakness. And if I did not tell Brenda, how was she going to know?

Open the doors as they come. It is better to contend with what's behind them together than by yourself. With Cabo experiences, they happen less and less over time because they can be disarmed so quickly. The risk was well worth it.

Ladies, once again I (Brenda) would like to speak to you. Are you giving your man a safe place to open a door? Is there a listening ear and a willingness to understand on the other side of the door? Do you give him a chance to really expose his feelings without being judged, laughed at, or ridiculed? Guys, this applies to you too as your woman takes the courageous step to open one of her doors.

For each of us, when we hear the words, "I have a door to open," we know four things are expected of us:

- I am all ears.

- I understand the significance of what he/she is about to say.

- He/She has my full attention (which means we stop what we're doing and give them eye contact).

- Then, I LISTEN.

Here are the conditions of listening:

- Listen without an agenda.

- Listen without thinking about what you want to say.

- Listen without interrupting.

- Listen without thinking up how to "fix" it (unless requested).*

- Listen with your heart.

Guys, when Brenda starts to share, and especially if it is emotionally charged, I always ask: "Is this a listen to listen or a listen to fix it?" I am clear on her expectations of how she would like me to support her. Women, this applies to you as well.

The reason we set these specific guidelines is simple. My (Gil's) ears cannot listen as fast as you (Brenda) can talk. Communication is a skill and an art form. Using these guidelines will help keep the playing field level and the interaction civil, especially if you are in a heated discussion!

When we have taken the time to open a door to each other, do you know what the results are? Our mortar is strengthened and our trust for each other is off the charts. As we use this catch phrase and the ones to follow, instead of saying "I love you," we say "I trust you." To us, that carries as much significance and power as saying "I love you." Open Doors are mental connections to the past.

Bare Wires

The next example we'd like to share is called "Bare Wires." Think of this as an emotional connection to the past.

Let's say you are out having a great time. Your wife makes a comment about a business lunch with another man. It's quite harmless, but it touches a nerve.

She nonchalantly goes on with the evening thinking nothing is wrong while under the surface you are steaming mad. You are frustrated with her and don't know why. You try to push it aside. By the time you get home and settle in for the night you go off in a fit of resentment. She did not think it was such a big deal and did not pick up on your attitude. Even more, she attempts to reassure you that it was nothing at all. It's just a business meeting and she hadn't had a chance to give you enough details to help you relax about the meeting. And, even more, it was going to be a group lunch with other business associates involved.

Oh, that's a Bare Wire.

Instead of going to bed, you "right yourself" and try to figure out what just happened. You apologize to your ife and then ask her to help you unravel the sequence of events. Being the insightful woman that she is, she offers a brilliant suggestion. She says to you, "Since your first wife left you for another man, these types of meetings, which were nothing more than covers for an affair, trigger old memories or 'Bare Wires' in you. When I innocently made the comment about lunch, the Bare Wire was hit and the chain reaction of emotions went on like a 1,000 watt flood light." In a perfect world this couple kisses and makes up like never before.

Bare Wires are an analogy. They can be a word or statement or an emotional trigger sent straight to your heart. Emotions are sent through your body like an electrical current. Sometimes they are accidentally found. It could be an innocent comment, insinuation, or gesture tied to your past, or maybe the "ex" factor. If the wire is still bare, it's

> *You and your spouse come behind your wall together.*

because it has been exposed to hurts, broken trusts, or unhealthy patterns. Even more, it will be susceptible to shock if put into a similar situation. Luckily, it's not a full circuit. It's incomplete. But given the right circumstance, the circuit will short and the shock will come. You must be ready for it.

Sadly, something or someone has frayed your wires. Now elements of suspicion, distrust, envy, broken promises, and disregard can set you off. When the coating is thinned or stripped around your wiring, your ability to cope and understand is hard to keep in check. You try not to be defensive or to withdraw from your new spouse. Keeping your emotions in check becomes a constant battle.

For women Bare Wires are connected to the whole fuse box. You touch one little spot of the frayed wire and sometimes you get more than a small shock. It can be a flat-out electrical arching meltdown of the system.

In the analogy presented by Mark Gungor during his *Tale of Two Brains*,[7] he explains that a woman's brain is like a super highway of pulsing mesh wires that all interconnect, each one powered by high-voltage emotions. Touch just one wire and an entire power grid lights up.

During a recent circumstance regarding Brenda's ex-husband, I (Gil) made a comment about how I felt, trying to practice honesty. Well, it back-fired big time. Little did I know that my honesty would bring tears and two days of Brenda having to process the emotions that were set off inside her.

Wisely, I backed off and did not make any more statements that could set her off even further. I was not into getting electrocuted! She later shared and identified the wires connected to an issue of abandonment. From there, she felt placated and justified in her views of me. Thoughts began running through her mind—that I was being a poser to a decree that further frustrated her. The myriad of issues linked to the main wire of abandonment – well, let's just say she was off to the races on that super highway.

Life will fray your wires and leave you with many exposed ends. Each one still has an emotional current running through it. Trying to repair and restore each one—one by one—is part of dealing with your stuff. Get this work done before you say "I do" for the second time. If you've been married awhile, and neglected working on your Bare Wires, it's never too late to start rewiring!

Even though it's your personal stuff that needs to be dealt with when a Bare Wire is discovered, it is another great opportunity for you and your spouse to come behind your wall together.

> *A safe place acts like electrical tape.*

Acknowledgment of the Bare Wire to your spouse allows healing. If your spouse isn't even aware of the Bare Wire, how can healing take place? **They don't know that they don't know**. Trusting and being

vulnerable to share in a safe place acts like electrical tape to cover the Bare Wire—to insulate it and bring healing and closure.

Christ can be your electrical tape in a way like no other thing or person on earth. Invite Him into the situation to restore it wholly. He is already aware of the occurrence and can assist you in the act of forgiveness.

We are not saying that a Bare Wire may not still get hit from time to time. It is a process of healing and deep counsel that needs to take place over time. What we are suggesting is to restore it the best you can, as the wires show themselves, so it does not infringe on your current marriage. There is an ample supply of electrical tape found in Christ. Let Him bring healing. Everyone has scars and they bring up different reactions in us all. To operate at full power, don't get lost in sorting out each wire. Leave the re-wire job to Christ and work with your new spouse who needs all your circuits connected.

When a Bare Wire is exposed and acknowledged, we will say to each other, "Oh, that's a Bare Wire," and we put our listening guidelines as described earlier into action. During our breaks at a…seminar or via the Internet, we will have couples share with us how these terms have impacted them. There has been one common storyline that the women share about their men:

> "He would get moody or angry and I would immediately think it was something I did, or something with one of my kids. I would rack my brain or ask enough annoying questions that things would escalate. Things are different now. When things start to ramp up, for either one of us, and we can identify where these feelings come from, it totally diffuses the situation. When my husband has let me know that I hit a Bare Wire, I can have compassion and understanding so I don't hit that wire again. I'm not on the defensive because I know he's not mad at me. It's connected to something in the past. We are able to work through it together and it has brought us closer." —**M.A., Bothell, Washington**

In some form or another we frequently hear from remarried couples who say they didn't think it was going to be like this, imagining that

somehow entering a second marriage was going to be bliss. Honestly, we thought the same thing until about two weeks after the honeymoon and the proverbial "stuff" hit the fan. So, take a deep breath. Pat yourself on the back for a job well done and get prepared for more issues that you don't see coming until they are on you like flies on "stuff." (Yes, "stuff" is translated to keep the language clean.)

End of Chapter Questions

1. What unresolved issues have you not dealt with from your first year of marriage?

   _____

   _____

   _____

2. Have you dealt with your past hurts? (53 percent of others haven't.)

   _____

   _____

   _____

3. The two key factors for marital satisfaction are communication and leisure time. How do each of you define leisure?

_____

_____

_____

4. A square, a hexagon, or a hypothesis? What shape is your Love Triangle? How can you make God more of the focus of your marriage?

_____

_____

_____

5. Are loyalty issues between the parent/child bond causing problems in your marriage? If so, brainstorm some solutions.

_____

_____

_____

6. Are you committed to being unhappy and miserable, or are you willing to change? What are you going to do about it?

_____

_____

_____

7. How can you help each other with your Open Doors?

_____

_____

_____

8. What is a Bare Wire for you? How do you react?

_____

_____

_____

Action Item:

Each of you pick a leisure activity you can do together! Be creative and daring!

> *"Marriage is that relation between man*
> *and woman in which the independence is equal,*
> *the dependence mutual, and the*
> *obligation reciprocal."*
>
> —Louis K. Anspacher

Chapter 4

"I Didn't See This Coming!"

Chapter 4

"I Didn't See This Coming!"

Sneaker Waves

Situational connections to your past. They are real and they are powerful. They are what we call the "Sneaker Waves" of life. We've all heard the stories, or experienced it first-hand. You're walking down the beach, jumping and playing in the surf tides, when an unexpected wave knocks you off your feet. Before you know it, you find yourself on your back, or worse yet, digging sand out from between your teeth. Watch out, these waves can also sweep you out to sea.

Out of place and unexpected are these dreaded Sneaker Waves. They come out of the calm smooth waters of life and roll over you. Whether in a moment with your new spouse or stepfamily, or just doing something that anyone would consider normal activity, the Sneaker Wave shows up and does its best to ruin everything.

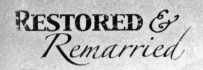

I (Gil) recall such an event with Brenda that left me dazed and confused. It's better told from her viewpoint:

It took place years ago, barely into our new marriage. We planned a "bonding weekend" with the kids. I think it was the first one. We have since coined these "Triple F Events." You know the kind—Forced Family Fun! Gil and I were excited to get away and start some new history with our blended family. It would be an incredible time to laugh and really get to know each other better, away from our daily routine.

Surprisingly, the kids (five with us at that time) seemed to be up for it. We set a positive tone going into it so the kids all bought into this fun weekend!

The location was two hours away, near Washington's Olympic Peninsula. Bruce and Vicky were gracious to welcome us with open arms to their lake house, not really knowing what to expect. There was anticipation in the air. During the drive we all acknowledged we were ready to hit the lake. The kids were all comparing their stories of craziness while water skiing. Kamikaze Kyle always has the best stories…and they are all true! Amazing that kid is still alive.

*T*riple F Events.

Once we arrived, we settled in as quickly as we could. We were ready to hit "fun mode." Everyone found their beds and I started unpacking. Then, out of nowhere, this overwhelming feeling crept in. I felt unsettled and depressed. At first I just tried to ignore it. I put my head down and kept moving. I was sure it would go away. "What the heck is this?" I thought. "Why am I feeling this way?" But the more I tried to ignore it, the more my eyes welled up. As I tried to hide the water dribbling down my face, I finally realized I needed to get out of there.

I made it to our car in the driveway and tried to get out of anyone's view. I just needed a place to re-group and sort out my feelings. I could

not stop crying. I was almost shaking. By the time Gil found me I was by the car. I couldn't even put into words what I was feeling. Not knowing what to do, I graciously asked Gil to find Vicky so I could talk with her.

> *I*t had all the makings of a Sneaker Wave.

As my dear friend and I sat in the driveway, I confessed to her what I did not want to admit to Gil. I was missing my "old family." I was supposed to be here with my ex and just our kids. What was I doing here with these new people? Where did *they* come from? Yes, I was grieving the loss of my previous family and the many fun vacations we had taken together through the years. But mixed in with the grief was a sense of guilt. How could I feel this way? Didn't I appreciate my new family? Look at how much the Lord has restored my life? I had an incredible gift given to me in Gil and his kids, wasn't that enough? How selfish can I be?

Talk about a combination of bitter and sweet.

My friend's understanding encouragement helped me identify the feelings. Once I was able to pinpoint what was going on I was able to move forward. I caught my breath, gathered my wits about me, and thought, "I need to talk to Gil." In the meantime, poor guy, he thought he did something wrong or that I was mad at one of his kids. I was able to explain to him what I experienced and we both agreed it had all the makings of a Sneaker Wave, hence the term. The power of the emotion (wave) is from the past. And it can knock you off your feet and take you out if you're not careful. You need to S.U.R.F. it together!

We learned about this S.U.R.F. acronym when we were leading a mission trip with Forward Edge International. While in New York City, "surfing" was just part of survival mode: S= servanthood; U= unity; R= relationship; F= flexibility. Every once in awhile we would ask fellow team members (especially if things were a little tense), "How's the SURF?" We needed to do a self check and look at the circumstances and the team as a whole. How fitting this is to use in our family now...and with each other!

You need to S.U.R.F. it together!

You have to ride out these Sneaker Waves together. I (Brenda) am not a water person. I am not very comfortable with water (unless it's frozen). But didn't we say in the beginning that stepfamily life is an adventure? What better place to be, uncomfortable, as a reminder that you can't do this alone. You need God.

Sneaker Waves are an internal struggle that sometimes catch us off guard. As time has been my friend, these torrents are fewer and far between, but they still happen. And they always come when I least expect them. So, when we get nailed and react by being quiet, a little more sensitive than usual, or flat out rude, we can say to each other, "Man, I'm sorry, I got nailed by a Sneaker Wave today." And you know what happens? All defenses go down. We are compassionate with each other and ready to walk through the scenario together. It is amazing how that affects our safety (mortar).

By exposing what just happened in your heart and head, it allows your spouse to ride the wave out with you and keep your head above water. Also, by being able to label what's going on, your spouse knows you're not mad or upset with them—you're just dealing with past issues. It's not about them, it's all about you.

Old Tapes/New Tapes

Behavior patterns are connections to your past. We are all familiar with the use of this common phase, but consider it in context of a new primary relationship of marriage or stepfamily parenting. There will be the need to change things up or approach the new environment absent your old habits.

According to reports, it takes a person approximately three weeks to reprogram the mind and body to take on a new desired behavior. That may seem overwhelming, especially if you have a number of old habits to break. For me, I just pray I live until I'm 100, maybe giving me enough time to deal with my faulty behavior patterns. But don't despair. Let's take on some of these issues one at a time, giving you a few examples from a remarriage point of view....

Scenario #1

Men, your wife asks you to take out the garbage. Sounds pretty harmless for the most part, right? It's generally the man's job to take out the trash in the division of labor scale of domestic chores. You go along with it to keep your wife happy, but after a while you start to feel a little like the butler or manservant. (*Brenda: Oh brother!*) Gosh, you get home and the trash bag is at the front door or by the garage door and the stupid garbage can is only fifteen more steps away. You begin to think that nobody else believes they can open the lid. Or, just maybe, they think you enjoy the smell. So, as an act of kindness, they leave the trash for you. They don't want you to miss your favorite duty.

How's the SURF?

Time goes by and the trash obligation attitude begins to build up. Emotions begin to well up inside of you. Thoughts begin to creep in, "I am the man of the house. Can't people pick up the slack here?

Can't they take the few extra steps and open the simple lid and put the garbage in the can?"

Because garbage duty was a sore issue in your last marriage, you blow up! You are reacting to how you interacted with your previous spouse. Something so innocent like taking out the garbage in your new relationship turns into World War III.

How do you take such a simple task in day-to-day life and "change it up"? How do you take it from an "Old Tape" and turn it into a "New Tape"?

Here's an idea. The trash detail is done at least every other day. Most families assign this to the lowest ranking child, but in my house I (Gil) have proactively taken it upon myself. I will snatch that bag right out of their hands. Rather than allow this legitimate request by my wife to get under my skin, I've turned it into a game that has become like an aphrodisiac in our marriage.

Not only have I served my wife, but I get to have fun with my kids as well. It's a way to mess with my teenagers' minds. My wife smiles. My kids look on in total bewilderment. "Why did he do that? Why did he get that reaction from mom?" Now, taking out the garbage has taken on a whole new meaning that we both enjoy.

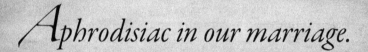

Scenario #2

Ladies, you are driving in the car and your spouse makes a lighthearted comment about your driving. He didn't mean any harm by it, but instead was just poking a little fun.

Since this activity in your last relationship often ended with you pulling over in tears or spitting mad, you feel like you are being condemned

and ridiculed for your driving. Rather than explain the tension because you may not know how too, you rip into the comment and become very defensive.

Horrified to ever ride with you again, your spouse gets out of the car and tries to understand what was it that he said that brought out the shrew in you. After getting the facts and actually listening to the sentiment, your husband, with your input, comes up with a plan for the future. When you drive, he gets to read the map and road signs and advise where to find the closest Starbucks.

When you're stressed, you regress.

Here is the point—you have got to retrain your relational tapes in such a way that if it takes three weeks or three months, you commit to change. It's part of the new marriage and family life together. Love is a choice and an action to improve and enrich one another's lives together.

Think with me about the rigorous preparation and training needed before you jump out of a plane. Hours are spent learning how to fold a special sheet of material (parachute) that will carry you safely back down to the ground. You also learn how to pull a release cord and a back-up emergency pack with a secondary chute. I've not had the experience of jumping out of a plane at 5,000 feet, but I've heard it is both exhilarating and stressful at the same time. That's cool for those who are into it. I'd rather have lunch waiting for you down below.

But think about this. What happens at 5,000 feet when the first parachute does not open could be a heart-throbbing rush for many. With their training, they do not panic. The next steps are taken as they have trained themselves to check the equipment while falling at 500 feet per second. Plan B kicks into action and the back-up chute unfolds and the ride down is tranquil. The same heart-throbbing sensation can happen when you are looking into the eyes of your new spouse, with an old stressful situation facing you. So the same question stands, what are you going to do?

For many, they go back to the old ways of dealing with things. Our hope is that instead you choose to take twenty minutes of downtime

to re-group. This is what "Old Tapes" are all about—re-programming your responses with a "New Tape." You need to be able to stop and think before you react to something that puts your defenses up. You need to recognize those "Old Tapes" and allow yourself to be vulnerable enough to say to your spouse, "I love you enough to be uncomfortable; I trust you."

> ## *L*ove is a choice.

Let's compare Old Tapes with Bare Wires. It will help us understand the differences a little better:

- Bare Wires: emotional feelings, reminiscences of memories or sentiments.

- Old Tapes: habits, actions, old ways of how things used to be done, expectations.

Remember this is a new relationship. It is a new recording so to speak. Get rid of the old heavy patterns and start fresh! Once again, your spouse won't know where you're coming from if you don't tell him or her. Even by telling, they may not get it for a while. Go slow, but for heaven's sake, at least get going. Start recording new patterns and habits together…today.

This reminds me (Brenda) of an Old Tape I needed to deal with several years ago. My ex was in sales. Although sales can be a lucrative career, your income is reflective of how much you sell. You can have a steak and lobster month or a rice and beans month. I think most women find security in knowing what kind of month it's going to be. There are those who can roll with the punches. In my old age I am moving a little more toward that camp. But early on, I needed to know what was going to be on our dinner plate that month.

I would ask (probably nag) my ex as to where he was with his sales numbers every week. He was good at what he did. But defenses went up and tension would build between the two of us. I'm sure I went overboard on the nagging meter. I felt my security was being threatened, but wasn't able to share my feelings constructively.

When I remarried, guess what line of business my new spouse (Gil) was doing? You got it. Sales. It was a different industry, but it was sales nonetheless. My previous behavior in this arena really wasn't on my radar until a few months into our marriage. I started asking Gil where he was with his sales for the month. He would nonchalantly respond, "I don't know."

I hit the roof. "What do you mean you don't know? How could you not know? You have to be kidding." It was more my attitude than words, but it quickly took a toll on our marriage. It didn't take long for me to fall into the same pattern as before. "Don't you know you need to track where you're at so you know where you're going?" It went quickly downhill from there.

This part of our marriage dance seemed all too familiar to me. This is where I used to get my toes stepped on. This is where I would take the lead. I have coached ice dancing, and as with any dancing, when there are two leaders, there's an awkward lack of cohesion. And when ice skates get hooked up together it's very easy to get cut. We're talking real blood and real stitches. It's not pretty. There is physical pain! And frankly, the marriage dance is no different.

The ice dancers who have finesse and are in sync achieve that because one person is leading and the other follows. It is an incredible feeling when you're taking the deep edges together through a routine and you trust the one who is leading. You become one with the ice and it's an art form to watch.

I wanted to have that finesse and be in sync with my husband in this "Old Tape" territory of mine. I needed to change my Old Tapes to New Tapes. Before this situation between Gil and I got too ugly, I shared with Gil my shortcomings and the dreaded Old Tape. I promised that I was going to watch my tongue before I blurted anything out in this area of finance. I kept my word and didn't "beat the dead horse" or

say anything about where Gil was at in sales. As a result, two very cool things happened.

We're not doing Old Tapes anymore.

Soon after, about once a week when Gil came home, he would pull a folded piece of paper out of his coat pocket. He would slide it on the kitchen counter, every time without saying a word. It was his calculator tape with all of his current sales totals. No matter how often he does it, it brings tears to my eyes. Words are not exchanged. They don't need to be. Through that same act he made it clear that my insecurities were heard and my need for safety was validated. That was the first "very cool thing" that happened.

The second "very cool thing" was that I was in a fresh place with the One who makes the sales happen…or not—the One who puts the food on my table. My ability to let go and trust my Lord put my heart at ease and let this financial stress not get between Gil and me. Who owns the cattle on a thousand hills (Psalm 50:10)? The Lord does! Isn't it amazing how a little trust can transform a relationship? I feel like I am in sync and skating with finesse again and secure in my New Tape.

Our attitude should be: we're not doing Old Tapes anymore. We're doing DVDs! Or, I guess now you might say, Blu-ray?

Foxhole

I (Gil) am a guy. I love war movies. I think in battle terms. My imagination sees bombs exploding, bullets whizzing, fighter jets zooming overhead, and tanks rumbling over buildings. It's just in my blood.

You see, my dad was an infantryman during World War II. He drove ammunition trucks with live stuff in the back truck bed to the front lines, then drove casualties and wounded back to the support lines.

Dad did not talk about his tour of duty much. I learned later it was for good reason. The last thing he wanted to remember was war. The pain and loss of life was too much to bear and not a happy time. In odd ways, the remarriage/stepfamily tour of duty has its Foxholes similar to what you'd fine in a combat zone. Maybe the risk of casualty is lower, but certainly the quality of life can get hit with shrapnel. And the battle of life can quickly take over your family. Here are just a few Foxhole scenarios.

Scenario #1

The phone rings and your ex is on the line. He/she forgot to mention they will be out of town this weekend and you need to take the kids. This was their weekend. You have reservations for a night in Portland at the Hilton and tickets to a show. This is not the first time this has happened.

The continual lack of respect that exudes from the ex is beginning to create a combat zone between you and your new spouse. Even though you've tried to get your ex to plan ahead and communicate better, things don't seem to be getting better. The ex was never good at planning ahead, and now this trait affects not only you but also your new spouse and new kids. You are helpless to change the pattern. So now what do you do?

This is a Foxhole!

Scenario #2

Your new spouse is dealing with situations at work. They lost their job, or they're looking for a job. All the while the rest of life is going on. The stress can cause conflict between you. This impacts your ability to keep a positive attitude.

This is a Foxhole!

Scenario #3

Drop off and pick up routines are often settled via the courts. Weekends and holidays are decided there as well. But your ex spouse does not uphold the plan. When you or your new spouse go to pick up the child, you offer some slack. The last thing you want is for the children to take the brunt of an unmanageable co-parent.

Coming up with options for kid transfers so they don't feel the discomfort is one thing. But your sanity, time, and sense of private space can turn into a Foxhole. Past positions of control between the ex and now the new spouse can be very awkward to work through. What can you do? A key is to put your spouse's best interest and comfort first.

This is a Foxhole!

By definition, a foxhole is a pit dug hastily for an individual to take cover from fire. These holes are regularly dark. You know what you are doing is not going to change things for the long term. Instead, all you are looking for is personal protection for a short time. Sometimes the hole is muddy and sticky. And most likely, there is no clear-cut option on what is the right thing to do. A foxhole is never comfortable. The situation or circumstance is too difficult for comfort. No matter how hard you plan or prepare to avoid these state of affairs, the "in the moment" is explosive for you or those in the stepfamily arrangement.

Foxholes are emotionally and relationally charged. They can be hurtful to those feeling stuck in the middle and trying to find peace. They can be a place of remorse because they are scary and the outcomes unpredictable.

Our suggestion? Dig in for the short run and ride it out. Hunker down together, out of the line of fire. Get some perspective. Then, when things have calmed down, make it very clear to your spouse that you're not going anywhere and you agree that you have each other's back.

May we remind you here of the Love Triangle and the principle it plays in your wall. This can be a strengthening point for a couple. It's an opportunity to grow stronger by protecting one another during the

encounter/battle. Whatever the situation is, watch each other's back and pray with the understanding that the Lord is in there with you.

> *You have each other's back.*

When either of us mentions that we are in a Foxhole we know exactly what that means. We kick our listening skills into high gear and begin to ride out the situation. Fortunately, most Foxholes don't need to last long because we learn they are part of the remarried/stepfamily adventure.

Phantoms

Do you struggle to grasp abstract ideas or concepts? As complicated as holding a breeze with your bare hands or bottling fog, I (Gil) am going to attempt to offer an explanation about an eerie phenomena. I'll use two examples to get the thoughts out in the open, and then you choose the one best suited to your experience. Interpreting something concrete that acts more like vapor is going to be a stretch, but I've got to share from my gut.

For the sake of definition, Phantoms or Ghosts can be photos, memorabilia, keepsakes, trinkets, or material objects that stimulate emotions connected to the past. Like a wisp of air, these uncanny gut punches are gone as fast as they come.

The first example, known as "phantom pain," has long been a mysterious reality for people who have had a leg or arm amputated. As I understand it, phantom pain comes from a limb that no longer is there. Actual pain can be sensed in a foot or hand that has actually been gone for years. Sensations felt by those who have experienced amputation express feeling warmth, cold, itchiness, or even tingling.

Phantom pain is not to be confused with the remaining stump, which truly does emit pain.

No matter what your brain does, it cannot cancel out the true feelings that are felt in a limb that is gone. Now think about this in the context of marriage. Do you see a parallel by chance with a spouse or parent who has been cut off from the marriage and family? Feelings or thoughts may still exist even though the person is gone. Memories sweep through your mind when an object triggers emotions of pain or warmth.

Secondly, there is the phantom past. Let's use the famous story of the "Ghost of Christmas Past" from *A Christmas Carol* by Charles Dickens. As it pounced to the forefront of Scrooge's dream life, the "past" woke him to the "Ghost of Christmas Future". Poor Scrooge was caught between his future and his past, depending on how he dealt with the present. As the story goes, this dilemma of changing his ways to become a more benevolent, compassionate man determined his fate, his future, if you will.

These ghosts were as real as life to Scrooge. In the same way, the Ghosts we encounter in moving into our present life of remarriage and stepchildren are vivid reminders of things from our past. Strangely, we have no idea how Ghosts of the past will affect the future until we're there.

Phantoms are lurking mementos from "marriage or family" past. Phantoms can also be emotional wisps that are stirred mystically. These random tangible material objects quicken the memory and can trigger either positive or negative feelings in all of us. Mysteriously, your response could be remorse, apprehension, feeling left out, or oddly warmhearted at the same time. Depending on how the reflection is associated to the past, reactions can be expressed obnoxiously by the one who had the encounter.

If you mishandle your response to the Phantom, it could be a slam against your new wife or husband. Worse yet, your reply could be an insult against your stepkids who are already trying to figure out how to adjust to the new situation.

If you ignore the Phantom you miss an opportunity to engage your new spouse or children and learn from the past. If you can reminisce favorably together, it solicits familiar spirits between you and the new family unit. Frankly, I (Gil) did not do this perfectly. But in hindsight, I think this is good advice.

Phantoms will appear when least expected! So how can you prepare in advance? How can you be ready to deal with it in the moment, taking advantage of the encounter? Don't be scared of the boogey man's impact on the present. Deal with the issue. Get it out of the shadows of your remembrance by not letting it grow into something larger than life.

First, share the experience with your spouse. Tell how the "appearance" affected you. Then listen to the history behind the Phantom. Acknowledge the past for the good times gone by, and then together decide how to remove or move the item or memory as respectfully as possible.

Take the object that was formerly connected to their previous family and save it for the child. If from "marriage past," let whose memory it belongs to choose how to remove it from the present. Take practical action for the one who got spooked. With love and respect for them, they'll know that a course of action for future Phantoms will be taken to control emotional fallout.

Take a glimpse at two of our many Ghosts that have appeared. See how we handled them in the moment. And learn how the action affected our future.

I (Gil) encountered the Phantom of husband and father past: i.e., Brenda's ex, when I was helping clean up the kids' upstairs bathroom. An old picture of the kids' dad was still hanging in an old familiar place which, for the most part, was no longer seen but had just become part of the wall. My coming on the photo was a complete surprise to me and caught me off guard—like staring at a ghost of the father that had lived here before me. For many years this bathroom had been shared by my three new sons while they were all under the age of twelve.

After our marriage, this bathroom where the photo was hanging would now have two new siblings zooming through it while my biological kids were over every other week. For my kids it seemingly would be odd looking up at a photo of someone else's dad and, at the time of the photo, a baby stepbrother. A very normal picture, but for my two kids, they confirmed it was awkward. It represented the Phantom of marriage and family past. And frankly, it was creepy for me.

I spoke to Brenda about the photo, knowing that it would be significant to her boys. At the same time it was setting me and my kids ill at ease. I sought her suggestions on how to deal with the placement of the photo.

Shortly after our marriage, we remodeled the house. As a result, we had more room and a place for each kid to have his or her own space. The photo then was placed into one of her boys' rooms. This action lifted the Phantom without disrespecting my new sons and set a positive course for future discussion concerning the Phantom of their dad in our house.

To give you perspective, we set up house in the home that Brenda and her family had lived in before her divorce. There was a lot of history of the Phantom still present at the house. When you start over, there are photos and keepsakes that may not have been cleared out after the divorce. As you come across these trinkets, the Phantoms jump out and create fear or anger or a variety of thoughts that interrupt your new happy household. You choose in those moments if the Phantom will disturb your marriage.

What's weird is, as the children grew up and began to move out, these Phantoms haunted them as well. Due to the past failure of their parents' marriage and the problems that remain unresolved, it carries over. We found that how they dealt with marriage themselves is a huge hurdle. Some have done well and others still struggle. They long for good marriages themselves, but the Phantom of what happened to their parents still hangs around like a ghost.

An Innocent Phantom

Another phantom that visited us was known as woundedness. My manhood in my previous home had been trampled. In one set of circumstances, a Phantom that had been long forgotten suddenly appeared.

Brenda was sharing her thoughts in response to a recent radio talk show about mild-mannered men. I requested her input on the definition of what it means to defend and fight aggressively for your wife. Her comment (which was innocent) caused a flashback to a crushing insult from my ex. It was an affront to my character.

I got angry, disrespectful, and vehemently defensive. I felt exposed as an old Bare Wire had been uncovered. It was like facing a Ghost of my past. *My character was being questioned again and I was the one doing the questioning.* Self-doubt reappeared, then self-assurance was dashed again like an accuser from my past. This Phantom was pitiless. I had dealt with it many times before, but could not break through the fog of my own fears to give it a crushing blow.

This old Phantom and all its implications actually turned on Brenda, which produced strong feelings of hurt and distrust. The very issues that were Phantoms of her past marriage were brought to the surface. Not stepping forward in a "manly" or strong attitude threw her into an insulting accusation of me being a poser! Please understand, I dread being a poser!

Together, we jumped into a Foxhole! The haunting was threatening us both. We prayed, we kept down, and quietly held steady. After a few days, the ability to be honest with each other broke through the old suspicions. We were able to take the episode of this Phantom's appearance and sweep out reservations that would break down trust.

Phantom Ping-Pong Player

A discussion happened to be going on in the garage one evening around the Ping-Pong table. I (Gil) was invited to stay and be part of this conversation between my new sons. I mostly listened, but my

opinion was asked for, which made me feel awkward and extremely like an outsider.

My reply required me to be transparent, vulnerable, yet brave—speaking from my mind and heart. The question involved my perspective on their own relationships to their bio father, especially as they pertained to matters of faith. The Phantom took the nature of "what if" our dad squared things away with God. Immediately, I was staring at the "Father of the Family Past." Honestly, I questioned my role again in these young men's lives, but with respect for them, I answered their question.

I expressed my doubts and uneasiness. I questioned my place to speak into their lives and of the "what if" concerning their dad. And, most of all, I wondered how it would impact their view of me. If their father were to square away with God, would they want me out of their family? Reassuringly, they all said no! "What is past is past" was the unanimous reply. In this case honesty won the day. I have a closer relationship with them and the Phantom of my concern has been brushed away.

We traversed events and episodes that caused the Phantoms to appear one by one. There are countless Phantoms that hold over from our past. But as we address them, using the terms we are sharing with you, we are able to chase them away.

Phantom pain is not to be overlooked as though it is not real. With proper handling, how to deal with the invisible influence can be managed. Our advice is to be careful as to how you deal with Phantoms in the present. This will impact the future. *The future is how you handle the now; don't let the past spook you.*

Short Accounts

A few chapters ago we talked about the walls couples build. The usual walls come between couples and can be twelve feet high and four feet thick. How does your relationship maneuver around something like that? The average couple spends six years building walls that are impenetrable before they attempt any kind of counseling. Six years!

How many couples realize what they have been doing to themselves or their relationship?

By implementing Short Accounts, we think you will save hundreds of hours of bickering and thousands of dollars on counseling bills! The foundation of Short Accounts should sound familiar to you. Here are the five points:

1. Christ: the center of your wall, at the top of your love triangle.

2. Commitment: my word is my word.

3. Close off all exits: no back door (to leave the relationship).

4. Divorce: a word never to be uttered.

5. Safety: is foundational to everything we are talking about to strengthen our marriage.

Short Accounts are about keeping the air clear with your spouse. Keeping the lines of communication running mean and lean...in a good way! Remember, you're on the same team, behind your wall. You can't let little things get in the way. Yet, you may hesitate to share because of Old Tapes or Phantom pain from the former spouse. If you share something that has been bothering you or that you are

You said I was fat!

concerned about, will your new spouse react the same as your ex? Is it safe to share, even the little things?

The longer you stuff it, the harder it will get. You know how it goes. You begin by thinking, "Oh, it's nothing." But before you know it, a lot

of "nothings" add up. You explode over something that is small and not even related to the issues at hand.

Think of your "nothing" as a sliver. Sometimes we get slivers that aren't very deep. They may hurt a little, but more than anything, they are annoying. Slivers are usually easy to get out. Sometimes they come out and we don't even notice. But what about the slivers that are a little deeper? So deep, in fact, you can hardly see them. They can be more than annoying, they are distracting. You try to disregard it and get on with life. You think if you just ignore it that little discomfort will go away. You might try to rub some ointment on to soothe it for awhile.

Your finger starts to turn red, maybe a little puffy and puss forms. Then, before you know it gangrene sets in and you have to cut your finger off! That sounds a little radical, doesn't it? (*Think about divorce.*)

Compare that to an account that has not been kept short; an ongoing comment that seems to fester. Your husband says to you, "Your butt looks big in your sweats." You defend yourself and brush it off. Then he doesn't take the garbage out. In the meantime he does nice things for you. You get snuggled into bed and in the middle of the night you need to go to the bathroom. You're still asleep until you fall into the cold water (you know what I'm talking about). You go ballistic!

Your husband apologizes for not putting the seat down and goes back to sleep. But you can't let it go. In the heat of the moment you say, "I can't believe you did that. You don't love me (pregnant pause)… and you said I was fat!" Your poor husband, who is really awake now, wonders if he has been on another planet! "What are you talking about? I have never said you are fat!" "You said my butt looks big in my sweats!" Whoa. Talk about a slippery slope!

Falling into cold water in the toilet in the middle of the night is shocking. But what's really going on here? It sounds like a sliver that got disregarded. An innocent remark was taken the wrong way, was not addressed; the air was not cleared.

Let's clarify. When an offense comes up and you want to express it, stop. Ask yourself the tough question, "How important is it?" We all know that comments are made or situations occur that we may not

like. We need to let some of these go. However, if there is something that keeps gnawing at you, there is an action you can take. Go to the Lord first in prayer. Allow Him to speak to you. This will slow you down and hold yourself accountable. The last thing you want is to rush ahead and start nagging. This goes for the guys just as much for the ladies.

I don't have time for this!

By the way, Gil actually did make the comment that my butt looked big in my sweats. After he saw the look on my face he clarified and said the sweats were all stretched out in the derrière area and it made my butt look big. Just for the record, my butt isn't that big…I don't think!

Not keeping Short Accounts erodes the foundation that you have been building to protect your relationship. As a matter of fact, if you say you are being honest, Short Accounts are non-negotiable. Without fail, when I (Gil) make an insinuation and I stop myself, Brenda will remind me about the rule, lovingly of course. Holding onto a fault breaks down the trust level. Because the safety in the relationship is at risk of being lost, holding onto a perceived offense is not an option.

Don't forget the foundations for your wall. They are Christ and commitment. By not keeping Short Accounts, you are allowing the opponents of your marriage to gain a foothold or create division. One of my favorite mottos that Brenda says is fitting in this setting. It is "I don't have time for this!" What she means is: "Let's deal with this and get on with life. We have far too many other things to accomplish, to take care of, and to have fun doing. Arguing or being upset with each other about any issue is just a waste of time."

We threaten (in jest and lightheartedness) to bring out the fictitious "pink padded 2 x 4" to whack one another upside the head. This is necessary to avoid the shenanigans of holding onto vital information.

That impacts trust, safety, and the loving relationship we are working to protect and enjoy.

The opponents of your marriage relationship are:

- getting distracted

- becoming discouraged

- feeling defeated

Your marriage is not invincible. The practice of keeping all issues in loving accountability is an asset. Short Accounts can be a starting point for healing and growth. View them as a positive thing. Short Accounts will bring strength to you as a couple! Consider these wise words…

James 1:19, 20

> *"This you know, my beloved brethren. But let everyone be quick to hear, slow to speak and slow to anger; for the anger of man does not achieve the righteousness of God."*

In their book, *Saving Your Second Marriage Before It Starts*, Drs. Les and Leslie Parrot refer to a practice they call "Withholds." By withholding information from your spouse you could be harming yourself or missing out on the love you really desire. Here is a brief explanation of how it works:

Three magic words…

Both husband and wife write down two things you appreciated that the other had done in the last two days, but you did not tell the other thank you or how much you enjoyed their gesture. Then, write down one thing that in the last two days the other had done that irritated

you. Once that is complete, each person takes a turn to share the information they had withheld until now.

The rule is that while you are hearing the withholds, all that the listening party can do is reply "thank you." That is all! Just "thank you." This allows the couple to share something that is bugging them without concerns of a huge blowout or defensive reaction. Couples are allowed to critique each other in the context of affirmation at the same time. (*Cool huh?*)

The Parrotts' suggestion is to eventually be able to say to each other, "Do you have any withholds to share?" Offer each other a moment to gather their thoughts and go through the steps. In time this is a healthy way to lovingly discuss a rough spot without a lot of squabbling.

Recently I (Gil) was returning an email to a young husband who shared that he and his wife were doing a lot of fighting. My reply to him was to look at James 1:19 and 20. As the man of the house, you are to listen with your heart and hear your wife speaking from her heart. Back up and look long and hard at what is really going on with the issue that is causing the disagreement. Is it a small thing you missed or that she missed? If it's a "big hairy mess" issue, then seek some help. For the most part, we've learned that a lot of small issues left unresolved turn into an avalanche.

In our first marriages we thought everything was fine. But then, bam! All kinds of stuff came pouring out that either could not or would not be resolved. Small issues became mountainous and from there the train was out of control (thus came the "train wreck" analogy). This now proves in hindsight a phrase worth committing to your memory:

IT'S THE LITTLE THINGS THAT **DESTROY** A RELATIONSHIP;

IT'S THE LITTLE THINGS THAT **MAKE** A RELATIONSHIP.

Let me (Gil) add one more tool for guys to use while listening to your wife. I don't know about you, but there are times when Brenda will tell me something with a great deal of passion. She is serious about the topic and I am making the best effort I can to understand the facts. But

a mental block is not allowing me to "get it."

Rather than act like I understand what she is saying in "womanese" I say, "Could you please walk around the table again?" It's like using three magic words for a husband to say to his wife, "Tell me more." Sincerely done, you've just told your wife that you cherish what she has to say and how she really feels.

Here's a review of the terms we have shared so far. If ignored or **not** understood they will create grounds for conflict:

Open Doors: a mental connection to the past

Bare Wires: an emotional connection to the past

Sneaker Waves: situational connections to the past

Old Tapes/New Tapes: behavioral connections to the past

Foxholes: in the moment/unavoidable conflicts

Phantoms: old mementos, trinkets, or reflections that require special handling

Short Accounts: a tool to reduce or avoid conflict

We feel it's an act of love and respect to learn these terms that have been shared and developed through our own experience, then put them to use in the context of a remarriage.

Love and Respect in Conflict

"Even the best relationships sometimes have conflicts on day-to-day issues." —**Emerson Eggerichs**, *Love and Respect*

Dr. Eggerichs explains in his book *Love and Respect*[1] that women are looking to be loved in the context that they are being understood and can relate to. He goes on to say that men, in contrast, desire to be respected for their worth and contribution to their family and to be admired by their wife. (We recommend reading this book and keeping

it handy for the marriage library and family development.)

We found an interesting five-minute survey that we picked up from reading Dr. Eggerichs' material. It's about feelings of love and respect during times of conflict between husbands and wives. Here is how it goes:

We ask the men first:

> In the middle of a conflict with my wife, I am more likely to be feeling:
>
> a.   that my wife doesn't respect me right now, or
>
> b.   that my wife doesn't love me right now

> *In the middle of a conflict with my wife, I am more likely to be feeling...*

With a show of hands, A or B? Most of the guys choose A—not feeling respected during a conflict. Not surprisingly, 81.5 percent of men choose A when Dr. Eggerichs did the more scientific method research.

Then we ask the women:

> In the middle of a conflict with my husband, I am more likely to be feeling:
>
> a.   that my husband doesn't respect me right now, or

b. that my husband doesn't love me right now

With a show of hands, A or B? You got it. The women generally choose B—they don't feel loved in times of conflict and the percentage is at about the 80 percent mark again. We realize women *like* to be respected and men *like* to be loved. But generally, men *need* respect from their wives, and women *need* to be loved by their husbands.

Here is where the path of marriage meets the hiking boots of application. Ephesians 5:33 states that a husband must love his wife and a wife must respect her husband. Love and respect are commands from our Creator who designed relationships to thrive and be enjoyable. Could it be that we have made this far harder than the original design?

Respect comes more easily to men. Love comes easier to women. It is how the male and female are wired. Sure, there are exceptions to every rule. But when a wife is careful to show respect and obedience to God, in turn her husband will stay connected and teachable. What woman would refuse those attributes in her man? When a husband shows his wife love, her spirit will be affirmed, or better yet, she will know she is cherished.

Dr. Eggerichs talks about the air hose concept, much like a deep-sea diver who has fresh air being pumped to his dive suit so he can breathe. Eggerichs parallels the concept in that women's air hoses must have love to breathe. In the man's air hose it must be respect. Without the knowledge of being loved and cherished in practical form, a woman will suffocate. In the same manner, men need to be respected and genuinely admired to breath in the fresh air their lungs of self-worth require.

The Five Love Languages[2] by Gary Chapman is another wonderful book we recommend. This is a brilliant tool for your relationships, even with your kids. For those who need assistance studying your spouse's form of air (a.k.a., love and respect), the love languages parallel that concept. The five love languages are: quality time, gift giving, physical touch (not sexual), acts of service, and words of affirmation. As simple as these may look to put into practice, we still recommend you read the material to get the depth of meaning.

End of Chapter Questions

1. Identify a Sneaker Wave you have encountered recently. What were some of the details/feelings of it?

    _____

    _____

    _____

2. Were you able to share the Sneaker Wave with your spouse when it hit? Why or why not?

    _____

    _____

    _____

3. Identify an Old Tape. What circumstances were you in when you hit the play button of that Old Tape?

_____

_____

_____

4. What's the best way to call yourself on the Old Tape to your spouse?

_____

_____

_____

5. Identify a Foxhole you were in lately. Were you in it with your spouse? Why or why not?

_____

_____

_____

6. What does it look like for your spouse to "watch your back"?

_____

_____

_____

7. Identify any Phantoms that need to be addressed. How can your spouse help you put them to rest?

_____

_____

_____

8. How short is your Short Account list? Let's get it down to a zero balance.

_____

_____

_____

9. What is the best way for your spouse to tell you that he/she has a Short Account to settle? (A few ideas: Just say it, with chocolate, glass of wine, the remote...)

_____

_____

_____

10. Husbands: What is one thing your wife does to make you feel respected?

_____

_____

_____

11. Wives: What is one thing your husband does to make you feel loved?

_____

_____

_____

Action Item

Take a nap; you deserve it after all the investing you are doing in your relationship!

"They say it takes a village to raise a child. That may be the case, but the truth is that it takes a lot of solid, stable marriages to create a village."

—Diane Sollee, smartmarriages.com

Chapter 5

Those People

Chapter 5

Those People

It was an exciting time for us as our wedding drew near. Although the date was scheduled for January and the holidays were right upon us, we survived the craziness (including the remodel project of the house and the last minute details of the wedding). Everyone seemed to be involved and excited.

With only a few days left to go, there were decisions made that we still don't fully understand. Specifically, a few of our kids announced that they would not be attending the wedding. Talk about an emotional upheaval—in the midst of an already emotional time. It was very hard to accept, but completely out of our control.

As the years have passed, there have been light discussions about those decisions. Apologies were given and received. I (Brenda) still feel so sad about the way things turned out. If trust and honesty were in play,

I think misinformation would have been cleared up. But sometimes we can only move as fast as the kids will let us.

Is it the end of the world that those children were not there? No. But it made it difficult to get things moving and form our new family foundation. Our kids are an important part of our new family, and each one of them plays a unique and powerful role. Gil and I want to renew our vows with all of our kids there. We look forward to that day!

As important as our children are, nearing the empty nest stage of our lives is something to which we've both looked forward. When we first got married we considered—only for a moment—about having a child together. This can be a hard call for those who remarry. We can see both sides…both decisions. And frankly, you need to do what is best for your family. We decided that it would really upset the apple cart for us, considering the unique dynamics of our family. We didn't want to add any more stress. We will say though that once we made the decision not to have a child, there was almost a grieving process we went through. We still feel it to this day.

When you are young, having a baby seems to just be part of the marriage process. It is how you show your love to each other, creating this new life together. For us, the operative word here is "young." We were getting up there in age and didn't think we'd have the wherewithal to keep up with a toddler, let alone another teen! As much as we know it was the right decision for us, we still feel a tug on our hearts when we see a baby. We exchange "that look." So, to appease that tug, we wrote this book. For all intents and purposes, this is our baby!

Getting back to the empty nest thought…. As this stage draws closer to reality, we reflect on how quickly the time goes by. The desire to see the kids and know what they are up to is enjoyable. It is satisfying when they drop by or call in with the latest developments in their lives. Even though we have been a blended family for only six years, the time seems short and long at the same time.

We have seven children between us. We lovingly refer to them as Those People. In times of frustration or bewilderment we'd ask, "What are Those People doing? When are Those People leaving?" In this chapter

124

we are going to talk about **your** Those People.

Our kids ranged from twenty-two to eleven years old when we got remarried. (Yes, we were crazy!) It was a house full of teenaged boys and one princess. Most were in the teen years or about to enter that wonderful stage of life.

It is said that joining a stepfamily or blended family is much like jumping onto a moving train! When you think about it, the tempo of a young family has time to build as the couple settles into their lifestyle. Then along come the kids and all they entail. The blended family, for the most part, has already built up a full head of steam. Barreling down the track from the very start, there's not a lot of time to adjust. New routines of a new spouse, married life, your expectations, and the impact of kids, plus more kids that you don't even know….

"All aboard!"

.6?

In Clark County, Washington, where we live, we took a look at the statistics of the average size stepfamily. The average—4.6 kids. Now, we're not sure what a .6 kid looks like, but we assure you it's most likely a teenager! Finding the average stepfamily size in your area is helpful. If nothing else, it reminds you that you are not alone. There are plenty of other families going through the same craziness as you.

The one statistic that did scare me (Gil) was the fact that the average father spends less than ten minutes a day in one-on-one time with his children. Now with the .6 child (i.e., the teenager)—who knows it all and has it all figured out—those ten minutes may be all they want or all you can handle. Be patient and love them anyway. The point is, dads, when you add in the factor of stepkids and often the transition between two homes, the time you have with the kids is precious.

It is so valuable to ask questions about their feelings, to share your love for them and how you feel when you have to say good-bye. I know that every chance I got in the car was painful and powerful. Times would go by that no words were spoken or there would be a flurry of

information exchanged. Outbursts of hurt or confusion would gush out other times. To listen or offer perspective or encouragement took a lot of wisdom. You also had to risk a lot in deciding what to say or not to say.

The pain that your kids are suffering and the sorrow you feel because of issues of the divorce and its effect upon them is insurmountable. Let alone not being able to tuck them in every night. I (Gil) have to believe this was hard on both sides. So, gents, I will strongly say this—use your ten minutes to the best of your ability but be sure your children know that you love them.

> *The marriage can quickly get kicked to the back of the storage cars.*

To make matters even more complicated, try mixing in stepdad/ stepchild issues of trying to find true concern and express true affection. It's important and complicated. These are not your kids biologically but when you said "I do" once again, the new kids became part of the package. Some of you shrug your shoulders and say, "I got it." But even now finding my place as a stepdad is a delicate matter where I ask questions or offer advice/instruction or correction and try to be careful not to overstep my authority.

Those People may feel like complete strangers and flesh and blood simultaneously because they are both one and the same. Stepparents, arm yourselves! There is plenty of material to read up on and find direction for stepparenting. We want to encourage that role, but not so much that it overtakes the marriage, because…

If you ain't got the marriage, you ain't got nothin'.

It's no easy maneuver to keep the marriage as the focus. Not only is the moving train at full speed, but there is this primary relationship of marriage happening as well. You wanted to remarry to enjoy companionship, but add in Those People and the marriage can quickly get kicked to the back of the storage cars. Total defeat can quickly set in with thoughts of "here we go again."

We found trust and honesty to be our default. When asking each other tough questions to keep the love alive and not be overwhelmed by Those People, the safety of our wall was protecting us. Things could be going along just fine and then something came up with one of Those People! Unknowingly they attack your wall.

Two Revealing Stepparent Questions

Brenda once asked me two questions. I had her answer the same questions concerning this issue of Those People.

1. How do you feel when I (your spouse) criticize your biological kids?

   Brenda: When you criticize my kids, I feel very defensive. Through the years I have defined myself (this is not always a good thing) by what kind of mom I am. When you criticize my kids, you are directly attacking that part of me. It can very easily put a wedge between us and chip away at the safety in our wall. I feel it is a direct reflection of me as a person. I also feel that you don't like my kids.

   Gil: It's a complete put-down to me when you criticize my kids. It implies that I've not done a good job. I also feel disrespected on my parenting skills. It damages how I feel toward you because I feel attacked. It creates distance that I really don't want.

2. How do you feel when I compliment your kids?

   Brenda: When you compliment my kids, I feel on top of the world.

Once again, I feel it is a reflection of me and the wonderful parent I am. It is very important to me that you like my kids as much as I do. When you compliment them, there is a positive connection and it feels great! Our marital team is stronger for it too.

Gil: It is like a pat on the back that I really want...makes me very happy that my kids pleased you and that they had done well. It gives me hope that we can have happy relationships in our stepfamily and that my kids were giving it their best shot. It draws me closer to you and increases my love for you because you see the good in my kids.

We quickly realized by getting the honest answers out that often the problems we were facing were not between us but Those People creeping into our relationship. With that revelation, we learned that our wall was also going to be our protection from those we loved—our own children, step or biological.

In the Kitchen

It has been said that there are lots of ways to cook a stepfamily! In cooking terms, you can "cook" or bring together a stepfamily by putting them in a blender, a microwave, a pressure cooker, or toss them like salad. In his book *The Smart Stepfamily*, Ron Deal explains the best way to cook a stepfamily:

> "I recommend the Crockpot cooking style. Stepfamilies choosing this style understand that time and low heat makes for an effective combination. Ingredients are thrown together in the same pot, but each is left intact, giving affirmation to its unique origin and characteristics. Slowly and with much intentionality, the low-level heat brings the ingredients into contact with one another.
>
> As the juices begin to flow together, imperfections are purified, and the beneficial, desirable qualities of each ingredient are added to the taste. The result is delectable flavor made up of different ingredients that give of themselves to produce a wondrous creation."[1]

I am hungry just reading that!

The Crockpot method of cooking a stepfamily truly works. Healthy stepfamilies take time to build. Sometimes we forget that each member of our previous family knew each other from the day they were born. I (Brenda) had missed out on the early years of my stepkids' lives. I did not experience their first word or the excitement of their first steps. I wasn't there to see them off on their first day of school.

I'm sure there were precious conversations with Gil's boys as they were driven to the fencing salons for hours of practice, or the many dance recitals in which Kara performed. Gil was not there when Daniel had his piano recitals, Patrick with his modeling, or the many tantrums Jeffrey had (which for the record he doesn't have any more)! Those foundational experiences we have with our own kids are just that— experiences with **our** own kids. And they happened over years, not just months.

So why do we get so anxious when our "bonding" doesn't happen so fast in our new family? I would like to think that most stepparents want a good relationship with their stepkids. We cannot forget that the recipe of time and "low heat" (intentional relationship building) is vital.

When I (Brenda) am feeling shut down or put off by my stepkids, I have to remind myself that I am in this for the long haul. They did not choose this whole divorce and remarriage as part of their life plan. They did not ask for these events to occur. Neither did my own kids. The adults involved put them there. Ouch, yes. But that's reality.

Short of being hit by a truck or Jesus' return, I am not going anywhere. I will continue to sincerely love on my stepkids no matter what. I am committed to their father and they are part of him.

My dad got remarried when I (Brenda) was seventeen. I don't think I fully appreciated my stepmom until I was a mom myself eight years later. Since her passing eight years ago, I think of her often and would have loved to pick her brain for what she went through having me as a stepchild!

Adjusting

Stepfamilies need time to adjust to new living arrangements.
Are they moving into their stepparent's home? Is there a new house
being purchased? Does everyone have to share a room? How many
bathrooms do we have? Bathrooms are a great topic of discussion.
How can one of the tiniest rooms in the house have so much more
potential for a fight than any other room in the house? I guess it
depends on how many girls you have!

Are kids moving into another kid's "territory"? Will the lines of
ownership be drawn and, subsequently, feelings trampled on? After
adding on to my house, Gil and his kids moved in. Although it is
recommended that you try to start fresh and buy a neutral place, this
wasn't going to be best in the long run financially or logistically for us.
Lines were drawn that needed to be overcome, and they were overcome
by honest conversations and time. The format of a family meeting was
very beneficial because everyone had a voice and was clearly heard.

There are a multitude of details involved in bringing two families
together. Trust and honesty must be applied in family situations so
you can have short accounts with each other and be aware of any
bare wires. This family is going to be around for a long time. There is
a legacy at stake. Let's keep things running lean and mean (in a good
way) and not get bogged down with new baggage on top of the old
stuff!

Stepfamilies need time to adjust to new parenting styles. Some
parents rule with an iron fist, others with a cashmere glove. Within
the same family, there can be different temperaments in your kids, so
your parenting styles may need to be adjusted to get the desired results.
Taking the time to earn the respect of your stepchild will pay off huge
dividends in the end.

I (Brenda) know there were many times with my kids early on that Gil
made the choice to bite his lip. If there was something my boys did
that upset him or that he disagreed with, he would come to me first,
without lashing out at the kids. By showing appropriate restraint of his
feelings in the moment, it paid off relationally for the long haul.

Stepfamilies need time to adjust to new rules and responsibilities. Do you make lunch for the kids or do they make their own? Do the kids ask before they go to the fridge for a snack before dinner? Who feeds the dog? What time is curfew? Who pays for gas in the car? We have found that when creating the rules for our home, having the kids as part of the plan is the way to go!

> *I*solation is the enemy
> of restoration.

If they are involved in the process of making these rules, they will own them at a deeper level. They will understand (hopefully) the reason behind the rules. Obviously, they may not always agree. And you still are the parent and have the final word. But what if the rules at the other home are different? Remember, you don't want to slam the other home. Acknowledge the rules there but reiterate that the rules of this home are just that—the rules at this home.

Stepfamilies need time to develop. Time and "low heat" are key. Building history takes time. Occasionally, we may feel like we have to rush the process. Unrealistic expectations we put on ourselves or the unrealistic expectations we let others put on us can be a detriment to the family. Everyone is watching and we can't make any mistakes. If we feel like things aren't going very well, we don't want to admit that we may be failing again. Embarrassment can lead to isolation. Don't fall into that tailspin.

Don't Be a Target

Isolated, you become a target for the enemy. The destruction of another family is just what he would like. Isolation is the enemy of restoration. This is where the 60/80 rules comes into play. Remember,

60 percent of second marriages (subsequent marriage divorce rates are even higher) fail within the first two years. Eighty percent could have been saved with resources and encouragement. If you know you need help with stepfamily issues, PLEASE GET HELP! Don't let your pride get in the way of keeping the legacy for this family strong! No one said this was going to be easy. The train, she's a movin'!

A wonderful resource we used with our family was the Flag Page.[2] Here's how it works. You take an online assessment which asks you fifty-six questions to find out what motivates you in life.

Are you from Control Country? How about Peace, Fun, or Perfect Country? What five motivations make up your Flag Page? Idealist, Leader, Deep Thinker, Sympathetic, Neat, Faithful, or Great Sense of Humor are just a few of the attributes this assessment can reveal about yourself. It shows you what is *right* about you! This is an easy tool to use for your marriage. It can give you incredible insight into your kids as well…especially your stepkids.

When you don't have the knowledge or life experience with them, these "countries" can explain a lot! If I am from Control Country and they are from Fun Country, we are speaking two different languages! The Flag Page will help you interpret country languages so you can understand and appreciate your differences. Now, we can laugh about how different we are, because sometimes we are different!

> *The train, she's a movin'.*

I would imagine that most stepparents desire to bridge those differences between themselves and their stepkids. I'm sure you feel that way with your own kids, especially if they are teenagers. The best advice we ever received was to let the stepchild set the pace of the relationship. When we force our own agenda and time frame on our stepkids, we all know it can be met with defensiveness, unresponsiveness, or flat-out

rudeness. This can happen because the child is still hurting. He or she may not be ready for the depth of relationship you want.

The kids can have loyalty issues with their bio parent (which we'll talk about in the next chapter). And maybe right now they don't even like you! That's OK. Here is a good rule of thumb—however old the stepchild is at the time you marry, that is how long it will take for the stepchild to accept you (or at least be civil to you). Understandably, this is a general rule. We realize in some stepfamilies members may get along well right away. There aren't too many differences to overcome and communication is good. Be thankful, very thankful if this happens for you, because that is not always the case.

An interesting story was shared with us that revealed how real this "age = acceptance" rule works. Mark had remarried when his stepdaughter, Lizzy, was eleven.[3] Their relationship had its rocky moments, but overall, it was tolerable. Mark always wanted to have a deeper connection with Lizzy, but she kept the relationship with him where she felt comfortable. He accepted that and continued to be there for her, affirm her, and love her.

Years later, Lizzy, now twenty-two, was engaged to be married. Anticipation was in the air for the wedding. Out of the blue, Lizzy called Mark. Comfortable conversation had ensued about the wedding and what the future held for this young woman. Then Lizzy said, "Can I call you Dad?" After Mark picked himself up off the floor he said, "Why yes, honey, that would be fine. Thank you."

He recalled how often he felt that he wasn't making any headway in his efforts to touch his stepdaughter's heart. Many times he felt his attempts were falling on deaf ears and a hard heart. Lizzy was finally ready for the deeper connection with Mark as a father figure. Let's see, how old was Lizzy when Mark married her mom? Eleven. Double that age, you get twenty-two. Ah...the rule in action. The key here is, "Don't give up!" Don't stop investing in your kids' relationships. What a sweet reward for Mark...and for Lizzy.

Crockpot cooking a stepfamily allows you to relax in the moment and enjoy the small steps your stepfamily is making toward integration. Low heat, gradual intentional efforts to bring the family together, is

working smarter not harder. It can be frustrating at times and you may feel like you're not making any headway. Stay the course, keep the train on the track, and have your conductor (Jesus) lay your tracks.

Been on a Date Lately?

In the midst of slow cooking our stepfamily, there is one area that we have tried to be very intentional in. This is very important if you have girls, but boys need it too. Every so often Gil would take his daughter out, just the two of them. It might be just for ice cream or for the annual father/daughter dance sponsored by our community. I (Brenda) would encourage them 100 percent. I wanted Kara to know that I supported her relationship with her father.

That father/daughter bond is crucial. The type of relationship your daughter has with her dad will shape her view of men and the type of man she will marry. (Now once again, this is in general terms.) Dads carry huge potential to affirm a young girl's inner beauty, yet he can crush her at the same time.

As a stepmom, I wanted to help nurture Kara's relationship with her dad. I would take her out shopping for the perfect dress, shoes, and of course earrings. It was a reason for us to do something together, too. Because of the hurt I knew she was still experiencing, I wanted to let her know that I was not in her life to come between her and her dad. I know that was a struggle for her and I tried everything I could to reassure her. I know that sometimes it was received and sometimes it wasn't. Even when it's hard, it's important for stepmoms (and dads) to keep reaching out in love.

Encouraging the bio parents to do activities with their kids alone also builds trust. How? You are building trust with that stepchild. They will realize that you are not the enemy and that you are not there to steal their parent away from them. Please, keep in mind the Crockpot mentality! You're in this for the long haul!

Another way I (Brenda) have tried to affirm my stepkids' trust is to support them with their mom. When it was her birthday and they were younger, I would take them out to help purchase a birthday gift for

her. Any time I could "come on their turf" to help them, I did. Once again, I wanted them to know that I am not there to pull them away from their parents. I care about them and want them to know that I am here for them.

One more thought. You can be doing all the right things to build relationship with your kids, bio and step, but if there are destructive conversations aimed at you from the other home, that does not negate the fact of still doing the right thing. These negative comments can undermine what you are doing. If you had to stand before Christ today, would He see your relationship with your kids as supportive, nurturing, and pointing the kids to Him? Stay strong and consistent with your kids. It's a battle for their hearts.

Sixty-seven. That's how many different types of stepfamilies there are. We're all different, but there are similarities that overlap. Once remarried, I'm sure you have heard this as much as we have: "Oh, you're just like the Brady Bunch." Yeah, right. We thought we'd lighten the mood here and test your Brady Bunch trivia (answers are on page 143):

Brady Bunch Game

1. What years did the Brady Bunch run on TV?

2. Who is the youngest Brady kid?

3. What is Mike Brady's job?

4. Who said this: "A few years ago, I thought it was the end of the world."

5. Who is Alice's boyfriend?

6. What is the family dog's name?

7. Was Carol divorced or widowed?

8. What do Bobby and Cindy do to try to break a world record? Why?

9. In the episode where Jan was sneezing, what was really causing Jan to sneeze?

10. What color were the Brady's kitchen counters?

Are any of you living like the Brady Bunch? We love what Ron Deal says, "The Brady Bunch lied!" They made it look so easy! How many of us have a live-in maid and cook? How many of our kids get along as well as all of Mike and Carol's kids? How come we never hear of or see interaction of their ex's? We don't know about you, but we're not living like the Brady's. Yet, in some ways, because of various adversities, it has made us stronger and more dependent on Christ. What a great place to be!

The trivia of a TV sitcom may be fun, but it is not an expression of real life stepfamilies. Certainly, some stepfamilies find moments of laughter and truly enjoying the experience, but reality would have it more like "When are Those People leaving?" or "Are the kids themselves anxious to get out on their own?"

Most stepfamilies I hear about remind me more of a battlefield then a TV sitcom.

Degrees of pain from good, bad, or ugly divorces do affect the children in different levels. Look around and notice that the youth culture in North America contends with huge side effects from the breakdown of the family. Children of divorce from all ages—be they five to thirty-five or older—in one way or another are dealing with the aftermath of divorce.

It would be easy to head off into the "Fatherless America" statistics or effects of single mothers upon children, but that is not the aim here. If you are into the gruesome statistics, take a look at the study done by Mike McManus, founder of Marriage Savers. The review is called *Marriage Savers Answers 25 Tough Questions*.[4]

All the time we hear that kids are resilient. In a way, that's true. But our kids are still dealing with the pain and issues of being in between or dislocated. Recently, one of my (Gil's) sons had an interview for a college entrance opportunity. When I learned of the trip, I offered

to drive him over to that part of the state. I wanted to be sure he was fresh and to encourage him, plus just hang out there and back. We traded voicemails to make the arrangements.

One of the voicemails was so touching. He had to tell me that he did not need me to drive, since he'd asked his mother first. He went on and repeated himself two or three times in the voicemail. He wanted to make sure I knew that he was not choosing his mom over me but that he had asked her first. It wasn't that he loved her more or anything like that. He continued that his mom had arranged to get the time off work to make the trip and he was so thankful for us both and that he felt supported for all we had done for him.

Really, by the end of the voicemail, I hurt for him. It was clear that he did not want to hurt my feelings. Just look. Here is a grown man still dealing with a pile of stuff that he did not create. Well, the end of the episode was that his mom was not able at the last minute to make the trip and I could clear my schedule to make the run over and back. We had a great time! By keeping him the focus, he's the winner for the long haul being supported by his mom and his dad.

Resilient?

Over the years, I (Gil) have learned a lot about kids. Let me just share a few things with you, especially as they pertain to Those People that are so resilient.

Researcher Dr. Judith Wallerstein[5] explained in the McManus study that approximately one million American children suffer the effect of their parents' divorce every year.

This twenty-five year case study showed about thirty million children have been affected by divorce over the last three decades. Half of those children will witness a second divorce before age eighteen. Cohabitations are as common as marriage and may be outpacing marriage as we near the end of the first decade of the 2000s.

Dr. Wallerstein found that boys are more affected by divorce, and girls are more affected by a remarriage. Children feel intensely rejected when

their parents divorce: "He left mom or she doesn't care about me."

Dr. Wallerstein points out that:

> "...Girls seem to fare much better psychologically than boys, yet, females have a 'sleeper effect' that surfaces later in young adulthood..."

> "...Ten years after the divorce, close to half the boys (now between 19 and 29 years of age) are unhappy, lonely, and have few, if any, lasting relationships with women..."[6]

Granted, these statements are lifted out of the study to make a point that 80 percent of kids adapt to divorce/remarriage in some fashion. It could be adapting by silence and internalization of their hurt and carrying on conducting family relationships the best they are able. Family is family regardless of how dysfunctional it may be. But there are others blatantly displaying rebellion and rejection of any meaningful relationship with others, let alone their parents.

Overflow of "family fallout."

But just think. That leaves 20 percent of the children not accepting the situation in any shape or form of healthy adjustment. Our culture is experiencing the overflow of "family fallout." For Those People, they may have chosen to run and hide rather than deal with the pain inflicted upon them. In the end, they blame society or take up some other scapegoat.

Ron Deal says, *"Divorce doesn't end the dynamics of family relationships; it reorganizes them into separate households."*[7]

We also learned that the ages of eleven to seventeen are the hardest to create bonds with and it takes a little longer to connect with stepchildren. We agree in full with that statement because most of

Those People were in that age range in our new household. Some were over the age of twenty and they were even more of a challenge because of the natural affinity to independence, let alone the new stepfamily dynamics.

We desired to connect with them, but by then they were beginning to pull away to be with friends and establish a life of their own. It's a natural development for young adults, where the challenge does not present itself with Those People who are of adolescent age. Little ones under the age of ten have a whole other set of rules and understandings that need to be established in how members of the stepfamily are addressed or referred to. The younger they are there is a greater opportunity for bonding.

Many of you have heard the phrase, "You are not my mom!" or "My dad said I don't have to listen to you." Younger children tend to blurt out these types of statements because they have not yet learned the fine art of muffling their feelings or how to be "stepfamily correct."

When these types of statements make it out of the mouths of babes, be they eight or sixteen, the attitude should be, "It's all about the kids." Keep your cool and get behind your wall to protect yourself and the remarriage. It may be time to have a healthy conversation with the child. Acknowledging their feelings may help defuse those comments:

"You're right. I'm not your mom. It must be hard not to be with your mom all the time. How does that make you feel? Tell me more…."

Showing the child that you are really trying to understand how they feel and what they are dealing with will bring defenses down. Then think how best to love them. Remember, they did not ask for this remarriage, and whether you've been blending your family for three months or fifteen years, adjust and be flexible.

The legacy of your family and children are worth your responding in love. You want to see life through with Those People, resulting in a healthier point of view and quality of life.

RESTORED &
Remarried

End of Chapter Questions

1. How do you feel when your spouse has "issues" with your kids?

    _____

    _____

    _____

2. How do you feel when your spouse compliments your kids?

    _____

    _____

    _____

3. List three positive qualities you see in each of the kids in your family (bio and step, in and/or out of the home).

_____

_____

_____

4. Which child is the most challenging for you? Why? If you were to put yourself in his/her shoes, how would they see you? If that view needs some improvement, what can you do about it? (Remember, you are the adult here.)

_____

_____

_____

5. On a scale of 1-10 (1 being low, 10 being high) where would you put the cohesiveness of your stepfamily? Reflect on the crockpot method. How does your family look right now? Are they being nuked in the microwave, creamed in the blender, or "crockpotted"?

_____

_____

_____

6. Whether you have been remarried a few months or several years, how has your family adjusted? Are there still areas of concern? What has worked well? Share with your spouse any rough places that still exist and make a plan to help smooth them over. (Ideas: introduce honest conversations with your kids to have a safe place to discuss these areas; family meeting; suggestions from family members.)

_____

_____

_____

7. What is the most recent incident with the kids that attacked your wall? As a couple, how did you respond? Were you more behind your wall together or out front getting shot up?

_____

_____

_____

Action Item:

Time for a date! Take each of your bio kids on a date. Where are you going to go, what are you going to do? If you're feeling really adventurous, take your stepkids out on a date! Build history, laugh, and get to know them!

Brady Bunch Game Answers

1. 1969-1974

2. Cindy

3. Architect

4. Carol said this to Mike at their wedding

5. Sam the butcher

6. Tiger

7. Not known

8. Longest teeter-totter session. Because they were feeling neglected, but they gained respect from their siblings.

9. Tiger's flea powder

10. Orange

> *"Don't worry that children never listen to you;*
> *worry that they are always watching you."*
>
> **—Robert Fulghum**

Chapter 6

Parenting

Chapter 6

Parenting

When you and your spouse vowed to love, honor, and cherish each other—face to face in front of friends and family—a new parenting team was created. Without the luxury of a playbook, you didn't have options spelled out to overcome the obstacles. Men and women, I (Gil) must confess that I was thrilled to meet my new wife. From the statistics that I've read, we are enjoying being in the rare 10 percent of remarried couples who have gone on to improve upon that which we already had. I now enjoy a fuller, more content life. And by God's grace, I did not settle for a mediocre second marriage relationship that would make me wish I'd never tried the married life again. And now, because I am content in my marriage, I am a better parent.

Stepping up to the task of being a dad and stepdad, plus becoming a loving husband all at the same time, really calls upon you to intercede for your new and existing family. Standing in the gap between your

bio kids and your stepkids, at times it seems the best you can do is stand still and believe you are going to survive. The "I'm not going anywhere" mentality is a strong tower for both you and your wife.

> *I'm not going anywhere.*

The former methods of who you were and how you operated hopefully changed during the transition of being a single parent to being married once again. Parenting skills are transferable. But caution should be used in how soon and how much authority you exert in your new home. You are Dad or Mom to some of the kids and a stranger to others. Go slowly, ladies and gentlemen.

Fatherhood Crisis

When the '70s hit, married life was about to take a U-turn, and it wasn't for the best. Free love and acts of consenting adults began to run rampant over the culture of the day. Divorce rates skyrocketed. Conservative values began to be questioned and were suspect of ruining our freedom. Fatherhood began to get the "H" beat out of it and disrespect for authority was the order of the day in "progressive society."

Depending on the culture you grew up in, the mother was seen as the disciplinarian while fathers were trying to just be friends. In other settings, fathers were to be feared. Children hid when Dad came home and the "iron fist" was very strong. Yet still, in other family models, the father was just mom's boyfriend and was not around much. From the cities, suburbs, and rural settings across the board, the true mark of a man was being smeared to a point of confusion. It led to what we sadly call the Disengaged, Fatherless Generation.

No matter how firm the efforts were made to maintain order in the family or to encourage fathers, confusion became a cloud over our

communities. The "no fault divorce" rules were eroding stability both in the secular and faith communities. Need I say more about family life in America, or the rest of the world for that matter?

How do you father in an environment like that? Most guys have such a distorted perspective of what a real man is that they would be happy just to survive. The easy route is to get lost in hobbies and sports. Or worse, go overboard and get lost in your kids' sports and miss the heart of the child altogether.

Honestly, with the rampant attitude of free sex and no responsibility, leaving child-rearing to the woman, is it any wonder that our nations suffer from such ills?

Men, you have entered a war zone if you have chosen to remarry. The zone is there even if the woman you have married is on top of her game. The two of you are in love. A fresh start is the outlook in your mind. But your own child (or children), along with your new children, need the strength and compassion that only a father can offer.

> *Men, you have entered
> a war zone if you have
> chosen to remarry.*

In your uncertainty, I (Gil) challenge you to do the brave thing. Step forward and love your family out of your weakness and failure. Reveal the fact that you desire to lead but may not know all there is to know. Tell them you will try your best from the advantage of your experience and knowledge. Then PRAY for wisdom for all you're worth!

We underestimate the pain our kids have endured. Even kids with intact families encounter loss, fear, anger, and dreams that have been

shattered. Growing up is hard enough, but if your kids must face off with the split up of their parents too—add to it the craziness of remarriage—it may be like a last nail in the coffin of their dreams. What level of expectation and perspective do they have as they cope with the unknown in the relatively short time they have lived?

Men, make room for Those People to experience healing and to process their grief. As we've mentioned before, they did not ask for the remarriage and all the upheaval in the first place. Give them grace!

> *We underestimate the pain our kids have endured.*

Make Room for Grief

Grief is a powerful thing. If you want to survive in this new marriage, you must acknowledge the grief you have experienced. Give room for others to process their grief as well. They may be gushing out words or actions of anger and fear toward you and your wife/husband. But don't be surprised. Dreadful behavior very often is a cover for grief that has not had room or time to express itself.

Have you grieved the loss of your previous family? Have you allowed your kids to experience the grieving process? Allowing yourself and your kids to grieve will bring strength to the family. We underestimate the power of unresolved grief. It can come out as fear, anger, depression, and rebellion. You may need to protect one another through this process. Remember, you are a team! Many foxholes we traversed as a couple had our children at the center of the issue.

Coming from a point of trust and honesty will make dealing with this easier. Maybe easier isn't the best way to describe this process; it will

be hard. But it is necessary to move forward. And it's OK. You have permission to acknowledge the grief you may feel.

Acquaint yourself with the stages of grief. You cannot walk someone else through their own grief without experiencing the process first for yourself. And depending on where you are in your own process, you may be behind your children. Be prepared. As a review, here are the stages of grief:

1st—Denial

2nd—Anger

3rd—Bargaining

4th—Depression

5th—Acceptance

The bigger the loss the deeper the grief. Grief does not travel in a straight line. These emotions will not happen in sequence. Think of it more like a circle. You can be feeling angry one day and depressed the next. You can hit the bargaining mode ("God, if I do this, then will You do this?") and then acceptance sinks in. Don't underestimate the power that your compassion brings to your kid's acceptance of you as a new stepparent. It does not take a lot of words to convey your actions. A few words of understanding go a long way.

Children will generally exhibit one of three behavioral responses to changes in their lives: they will act out, withdraw, or become the responsible manager of the family. Many think that the third option is the most dangerous. The child who is acting out will get attention, if only a reprimand. The child who is withdrawn will probably get attention from someone who cares about him/her. But the third child will more likely be commended for taking on adult responsibilities or excelling in school. People assume that he is doing fine though he may not be ready for these tasks. Sometime later in life, this house of cards may well collapse, for the child has been maintaining the appearance of maturity while the substance of confidence and self-awareness is absent.[1]

Grief takes time. It is a process of letting go of something familiar and taking hold of something new. At each stage of emotional and cognitive development, the child understands the universe with more maturity. For children, the grieving process may not end until they reach adulthood. Everything you say now is like a building block so they will understand it better when they are older. It's important to tell the clear, concise, age-appropriate truth.

> *You have permission to acknowledge the grief.*

Teens grieve deeply, but often work hard to hide their feelings. Fearing the vulnerability that comes with expression, they look for distractions rather than staying with the grief process long enough to find real relief. Red flags to look for are anger, guilt, substance abuse, skipping school, dropping grades, and acting out sexually.

Keep the lines of communication open. Don't ever say, "You shouldn't feel that way." Listen to their concerns. God cares about how we handle our circumstances. He cares, and He gives us peace when we ask for it. He doesn't change. He establishes our feet in secure places.

The Most Famous Stepchild

Let's take a quick detour for a second. Ponder, with me, this question. Who is the most famous stepchild? In their book *God Breathes on Blended Families,*[2] Moe and Paige Becnel unpacked a thought I would have missed had I not become a stepfather.

Jesus is the most famous stepchild! Really, it's true. Think about it. Jesus was a stepchild to Joseph. He was part of a blended family. When that fact was pointed out to me, it blew me away. Think about that for

a moment. Being a stepdad can be intimidating enough, but to be a stepfather to the Son of God? Now that set me back. In Luke 3:23(b) it says, *"He (Jesus) was the son, so it was thought, of Joseph."*

Here is the storyline of Joseph's relationship to Jesus:

Joseph's initial reaction was threefold:

1st—"It's not my child!"

2nd—He planned to send Mary away quietly with as little publicity as possible.

3rd—There was great confusion on Joseph's part. How could this be happening. Mary had been promised to him and, by custom, they were in close relationship in preparation for marriage. When and why would she slip away for an inappropriate relationship with another man? I'd say he was more bewildered, and most likely not a little angry!

Then the angel who appeared to Mary pays Joseph a visit too. He offers an explanation for what is happening—to set the guy at ease a bit before he does something rash. The angel explains that the child is from God and the conception was in the miracle category. Mary had done nothing immoral. Further, Joseph is instructed to marry her and make her an honorable woman. Her life would be at stake if he did not step in and do the right thing. Add to all this the clear instruction that Joseph was to name the child Jesus.

Now Joseph's legacy is at stake here as well as a given responsibility to name Jesus. Naming a child was a role of the "natural father" in Israelite custom. Think about it. Joseph did not change the identity of Jesus by giving Him a new name. He took the circumstances handed to him and went with it. He raised the boy as his own.

Can you image knowing, as the stepdad, who the biological dad was and what consequences you would answer to if you screwed up? If truth be told, what kind of outcome would there have been when they were on their way back to Nazareth and realized Jesus was not to be found in the caravan home? Remember the story? Jesus is back at the

temple discussing deep theological stuff with the religious elite when Mary and Joseph find Him. What do you think would have been the upshot had Joseph said to Mary when they were halfway home, "Hey, go back to Jerusalem and get *your* kid!"?

Consider the providence of God by appointing Joseph as stepdad. Take that vantage point with your stepkids. It could help adjust your attitude. Maybe, just maybe, even though divorce and remarriage is not the best thing overall, if you take the position handed to you, you could have a hand in shaping a life for Christ rather than see one more child become a statistic of the outcomes of divorce.

Stepdads and stepmoms, you are being given a fresh game plan. Remember you are on the same team. When you signed onto this via your vows to love, honor, and cherish, Those People became part of the lineup. Immediate results will not show up! Accept that fact before you start. It will help you relax and enjoy—as well as endure—the journey ahead.

Now you can include one more phase to our byline...

> *If you ain't got the marriage, you ain't got nothin'.*
>
> *—Plus—*
>
> *I am not going anywhere.*

Co-parenting

I (Brenda) remember the first time I heard the term "co-parenting." I was sitting in the bleachers watching Daniel play baseball. A fellow mom was sharing about how she and her now divorced husband had this wonderful co-parenting plan. I literally thought I was going to throw up. Co-parenting? You've got to be kidding! It sounded more like a business agreement than two loving parents raising their children. Well, here I am today, working through the co-parenting issues myself. And the key to a successful co-parenting plan is "keep it to business."

It's funny to think that people get divorced because of things that drive them crazy about their spouse. Getting a divorce, they think,

will solve all the problems. They won't be around to drive them crazy anymore, right? Wrong. Now, as a divorced couple, the exact things that drove them crazy will not only be at an elevated level, but at a higher emotional threshold too. Add to it the fact that most of the time the kids will be the ones to take the brunt of the discussions between the biological parents.

Your Ex: What Type Is He/She?

The Good Divorce,[3] written by family researcher Constance Ahrons, has a wonderful guideline to identify ex-spouse/co-parent relationships. Below are some high points of her research. What type of relationship are you living with your ex?

Perfect Pals:

- High interactors/high communicators

- Consider yourselves best friends

- Interested in each other's lives

- Holding on to the old relationship

Cooperative Colleagues:

- Moderate interactors/high communicators

- Cooperate well on issues with the kids

- Resolve issues or avoid them

- Compartmentalize the relationship

Angry Associates:

- Moderate interactors/low communication

- Anger every time they interact

- Anger spreads to kid issues

Fiery Foes:

- Low interactors / low communication

- Ex spouses rarely interact

- When they do, they fight

- Need a third party (lawyer, friend) to help communicate

Dissolved Duos:

- Discontinued contact entirely

- Maybe left the geographical area

Does the previous list give you some perspective? Although you may be Fiery Foes and desire to be Cooperative Colleagues (the healthiest choice), who has control over the relationship? You cannot make your ex be one way or the other, but you can control how **you** interact.

As much as you would like a working relationship, that idea may be received with manipulation and not-so-nice words. Keep in mind, sometimes your new spouse can interact better with your ex than you can. Whatever arrangement works, if it keeps the lines of communication open and keeps the kids out of it, do it! And continually ask yourself, do I want to die on this hill? Is it really worth it?

As we have talked about the co-parenting relationship we have created two new categories: tri-parents and quad-parents. What happens when your ex's partner voices their opinion? Is this good or bad? It depends on the relationship between everyone. If it benefits the child/children involved, it's a good thing. If not, the bio parents need to agree on the boundaries, and stick to them.

We're all for healthy adults encouraging our kids, but if it is not beneficial to the kids, it's time to pull the plug. And remember, what happens in the other household is out of your control. You just have to learn how to deal with it. If your ex is not cooperative in an agreement with the level of involvement their partner/spouse has with your child, you may only have one place to go—one thing you can do. Get on

your knees and pray. Pray for the emotional, spiritual, and sometimes physical protection of your child. It can be heart wrenching to have to take your child back into an environment (after being with you) that you know is detrimental to their well being. But you're not in this alone. You have a heavenly Father who loves your kids too. In fact, He loves them more than you do.

Cut and Cauterize

Separation from the former marriage is a longer process than most people might think. As we interact with other couples, we hear complaints about how the husband/wife will still have some connection to their former spouse. Of course this causes the new husband/wife some concern and disrupts the relationship, even though the connection may be revolving around the kids or some unfinished business.

The excuses may be valid if he/she has better availability to the kids— if there is a tug of war of time in order to see them. As difficult as it is, the clear-cut separation of time spent at your own home concentrating on your new marriage should be the priority. There is a painful yet useful practice I (Gil) put into action early on that made this process easier. It made it so that when the time came to be in a healthy place for myself, let alone with my new wife, I had done the internal work necessary. It's what I call cutting and cauterizing.

Cutting and Cauterizing is a necessary step to healthy co-parenting relationships. My children are still my ex-wife's children too and that is the only connection that holds our relationship together. That one factor alone will cause our paths to cross now and then. When the children were younger, the frequency of connection was higher due to their age, activities, and our parental involvement in their lives. It's something you just can't get around.

When those situations presented themselves, we went to support the child in whatever they were doing. Fees or financial matters came up and would be handled by phone or email. The less interaction we had, the more tolerable the situations were. At a function together, the polite thing was to interact with the child separately and if in close proximity, to be polite and keep any negative comments to oneself. It's

not easy, but it's important.

As you can imagine, even in this section I find it important to respect my ex-wife. It is not good to dwell on past hurts or emotional scars. That is in the past, and we must do our best to leave them there—for our benefit and for the benefit of our children. We all know it is seldom easy to deal with one's ex as diplomatically as it sounds. And as cold as it may seem in how we have dealt with each other after the divorce, it has still been tough on the children.

For me (Gil), the focus switched the day I decided to ask Brenda to be my wife. When she accepted the proposal, our attitudes had to change. We had to come to terms with the implications of how our new life together would affect all involved. For our children, as well as our new spouse, our new attitude must be, "We're not going anywhere for the rest of our lives, til death do us part."

Getting back to the "cut and cauterize" concept, let me elaborate on the process a bit more for you. Principally, each person should apply this course of action before considering remarriage. If you did not take the procedure to heart (and I mean that quite literally) before you remarried, take time to do it as soon as you can. Think with me about the concept in how it applies to your emotional state of being—your full ability to give undivided attention to the here and now.

The best illustration I can offer is the process where a man's reproductive organs are "cut and cauterized." Yes, I am talking about the BIG V. This does not mean the man can no longer perform; he can just no longer produce.

With that picture in mind where a clean cut has been made then burned, the tissue melts and there is no longer any channel open. "Closed for business" is the conclusion. Any further interpersonal relations will not produce offspring. Are you getting my drift here? Any connections you once had to the former spouse are cut and cauterized completely. Better put, there are no jagged ends left to have any attachments.

How do you do that, you may be asking? The method I employed was going back to old places that once were shared—significant locations. Memories and events took place at these sites that were good and bad.

I wanted to be whole and I wanted my whole heart back as much as possible. It wouldn't be easy, especially after two decades of marriage and children. I wanted, and needed, to be healed in mind and heart! To reach this goal, I had to identify and face the bonds that tied me together with my ex, now cut off and never to be retied.

For me, I needed to dig down as far as I could. I needed to be reminded of the joy, or pain, of each one of those moments and say, "Good-bye." Tears and prayers helped to cauterize the steps that I was taking to regain a healthy relationship with myself. (Good grief, after attempting to hold one's marriage together for four years and failing, there's a ton of guilt and remorse attached, a lot of places to cover.) Often, I would get the opportunity to travel or be at a place that I had forgotten about, and there I would be alone crying and praying and saying good-bye. Relief, repentance, and reconstruction were happening all at the same time.

I don't know about you, but I felt like I had been torn apart—like two pieces of plywood that for years had been glued together. I felt literally peeled and pulled apart, with nothing but splitters and shreds left to make me who I am. As painful as it was to square off with the past, I'm glad I did. Now the triggers that would have set me off or make me feel defeated are easier to manage. Now, I can dismiss the negative connections and move on with my new life.

> *No jagged ends left to have any attachments.*

Believe me, going through the "cut and cauterize" steps were some of the hardest days of my life. I could have chosen to back off, but the more I pressed into the pain the quicker the emotional bleeding stopped. I could focus more clearly on my kids and rely more intimately upon Christ as I moved forward.

It made all the difference when my internal stability was called upon. Zeroing in on my shortcomings, and the mortal blows I had taken, allowed me to find my feet again. I could stand up and know that Christ would hold me steady. My confidence returned, even though it was challenged frequently by the cast of actors who had brought the former marriage to its demise.

I could now act and think with an attitude of forgiveness. And that was the key to fully understanding and realizing my completion in the "cut and cauterize" progression. The most difficult chapters of the process are, I pray, behind me. Of course, some issues still surface when I least expect them, but now I know what to do.

> # *When you slam your ex, you are slamming your child.*

As a result of this proactive approach to my past, the number of bare wires that Brenda found when we married was greatly reduced. Any issue was open for discussion. And if it needed to be cut or cauterized, I was willing. To enable new growth in our friendship, and eventually in our marriage, both of us needed to be devoted to the process. And then, of course, there was Brenda's side of the story. She had her own past, her own hurts, her own "cut and cauterize" process to go through. For those, she had to face them herself.

There was one instance that occurred about three months after we married that emphasized some failure to cut and cauterize. Something as simple as a birthday card to her ex-husband pushed me to be honest. I had to step out and trust that by sharing an issue that I thought needed to be cut I would not be misunderstood. I called her on the intention and asked how she would feel if I would send a birthday greeting to my ex-wife.

If I may, let me share my (Brenda's) side of the story here. When I married Gil, it wasn't as if I had one foot with him and the other still with my ex. This is just how I am wired. I am a very loyal person, sometimes to a fault. I send birthday cards to everyone. It's just something I do. In fact, I shared with Gil the other day that I have imposed a new ten-year rule. If I don't hear from someone, or if they haven't reciprocated in ten years, I will stop sending cards. Ten years! A little loyal? OK, I'm guilty!

If I send a birthday card to my ex, there wouldn't be any feeling attached. There wouldn't be anything behind it, which is why I didn't think it was such a big deal. But—here is the important part—because Gil was uncomfortable with me sending the card, that was enough reason for me not to send it. I may not agree with him. He may not totally understand where I'm coming from. But any reasonable request should be granted to your spouse if he/she is uncomfortable, especially in dealing with an ex.

I've seen too many couples get stuck with their pride to put something like this before their spouse. Talk about having your wall come *between* you! Aren't you supposed to be looking out for what is best for your marriage? What hill are you willing to die on? What hill are you putting your relationship on?

Feelings for a former spouse—be they anger, guilt, or a fond memory—are realities that should be dealt with with your new spouse in the healthiest, most open fashion possible. Nothing will impede trust and honesty quicker than such unfinished business. Plus, the effects upon the children in how you handle things are ultimately for their well being. Co-parenting will be tough. Yet if you take the time to be in the best place you can for your kids' sake, in the long run there will be a positive payoff for your efforts.

Kids will end up in the middle of the co-parenting relationship whether you like it or not. When there is unfinished business and game playing with your spouse, the kids are the first to feel it. It took me (Gil) a while to get to the positive side of this issue, so there is no condemnation coming from me. But parents must not place their kids in the middle, acting as messengers, spies, or peacemakers. It may sound obvious, but

this does happen, even subtly. We are to be the adults. The children, regardless of their age, are not equipped and should not be expected to take on such roles.

Find a method to communicate with the ex that works for you *and* them. Keep it as simple as possible. Deal with one issue at a time. If you are on your guard then they most likely are too. And at all costs, avoid getting the kids involved. Where there once was a team working to raise the kids, now there is division, and you can bet that the kids know it. Encourage the children to respect the other parent, even if you don't agree with the choices they are making. The more respect developed in communicating with one another while dealing with the kids, the better. There is so much to disagree about. Try to set it all aside and make the best decisions for the children.

It is crucial to support our kids where they are emotionally. They must be reassured to know that they were not the cause of the divorce (or the death of their parent). As they grow and mature, this subject may need to be revisited and information shared at age appropriate times. You don't want to keep bringing the subject up if there isn't a sign that it needs to be talked about. In many situations kids move on. They accept what has happened and it's not on their daily radar. Hone your listening, observing, and sensing capabilities to understand what is needed and when.

Other kids may deal with the harsh reality of the situation on a daily basis. They have underlying hurt and confusion that still haunts them. You should be the expert with your kids and know their heart. Trust and honesty should be the firm foundation in your parenting relationship. The goal is to provide a safe place for your kids to talk about how they are feeling. When conversations turn to the topic of your ex, be gracious in your comments, yet speak truth. Remember, the other bio parent who is out of your home is part of your child too. When you slam your ex, you are slamming your child. Above all, pray for wisdom and let the Lord direct your conversation.

Betrayal Factor

It has been said before that the stepkids should set the pace of the

relationship with stepparents. The betrayal factor is one explanation for this rule of thumb, many times impeding the growth of that new and tenuous relationship. You have heard it said that blood is thicker than water. It's true. And family ties are incredibly strong. If your stepchild has a close relationship with you (the stepparent), they may feel they are betraying their bio parent. I can only imagine the internal struggle a child would have, especially if the bio parent is not supportive of this new relationship. Bottom line—the stepparent cannot control the bio parent. They can only monitor their own words and actions.

Never is there a better time to review—and memorize—Philippians 4:8, "...*whatever is true, whatever is honorable, whatever is right, whatever is pure, whatever is lovely, whatever is of good repute, if there is any excellence and if anything worthy of praise, let your mind dwell on these things.*" Your stepkids need to hear this from you. You are to be a healthy parent role model, no matter what you are up against.

You can have a bio parent who is strung out on drugs or in and out of jail. Their child will be loyal to them no matter what. Kids may feel they are the rescuer and feel greatly needed. The "needy" bio parent can easily play into this with their child and influence situations to win and/or keep the love of the child. This behavior is full of manipulation and insecurities on the part of the adult involved. It's a lot of wasted energy too.

No matter what type of relationship your stepchild has with their bio parent, you need to know your place in the situation. We made it clear to our stepkids early on that we were not there to replace or take over the position of their bio parent. We are here to support them and be one of their biggest cheerleaders in life! Affirming their relationship with their bio parent gives freedom to your stepkids.

The last thing you want to do is put your stepchild in a position where they feel the need to guard or defend their bio parent. Now, will some kids automatically defend and guard their bio parent? Of course. But coming alongside them and keeping a positive, supportive attitude will help a ton. This may take time, but that's OK. You're not going anywhere, right? And remember, your stepkids are watching your actions and attitude whether you use words or not.

On the other hand, the bio parent needs to let the child know that it is OK to love the stepparent in the other home, if there is one. This is especially true if there is a tender relationship building. Feeling threatened by another adult in our child's life can rob that child of experiences and points of view that will benefit their growth in the long run. Our desire should be that our children have as many healthy adult relationships in their life as possible.

If the stepparent relationship is not the healthiest, and communication is strained at best, how is that going to help your child? Putting the child's needs aside for a moment, isn't this a great opportunity for you (the stepparent) to sharpen your Philippians 4:8 skills? Strive for respect, trust, and honesty in the relationship. As the child grows and has to interact with different people in their life, he/she will gain the skills they need to communicate respectfully with people who may be hard to deal with or have opposing views on life. First and foremost, your job is to model healthy behaviors.

When the kids are younger and you recognize unhealthy parenting in the other home, you need to step in and be the voice of the children. But, as they grow older, your kids may need to navigate these "battles" on their own. You can offer your help and wisdom from the sidelines. The focus is not to have the kids carry any more heartache than they need to. We'll talk about this more in a moment.

At times, circumstances are totally out of our control. But they are not out of Christ's. Put your kids at the foot of the cross and let go.

We found it became rather awkward at social gatherings or sporting events with our stepkids when it came to introducing them to friends. Do you say, "This is my stepson; this is Gil's daughter; this is my son; this is my bonus kid," or just plain, "This is Kyle?"

We had conversations early on and asked our kids how they would like to be introduced. I (Brenda) didn't want to disrespect their mom by calling them "my kids." Yet I didn't want to alienate them by using the "step" word. We went with whatever term they felt most comfortable with. It really didn't matter to me. My concern was that they felt valued and respected. And it is an incredible honor when our stepkids introduce us as "the parents" or, sometimes, Mom or Dad.

There is another betrayal factor that needs to be acknowledged. If the stepparent is finding their relationship with the stepchildren growing, there can be loyalty issues with their own kids. Thoughts of "If I engage my stepkids I am cheating on my kids" can rob everyone involved. What about the bio kids seeing their parent connect with their stepsiblings? How will it make them feel? This is very touchy territory, and as a result it's important to affirm your bio kids. They will never leave their "spot" in your heart. They need to know that. If your stepchild opens the door for relationship, please walk through it, especially if their relationship with their bio parent who is outside of your home is suffering.

Strings & Buckets

Kids simply want to be connected to the people they love, no strings attached. The messages adults give children in an attempt to gain their loyalty in effect are strings of manipulation. One couple shared with us a story of an event that took place with one of their kids:

A school dance was coming up for their daughter. The father and stepmother were excited and supportive for their teenage girl to attend. They wanted to participate and welcomed their daughter to bring her friends over after the dance for food and a movie. The girl and her friends had prepared for the dance at her mother's home. The dad and stepmom wanted to participate in their daughter's life and to get to know her friends better.

As the story progressed, the daughter chose to have her friends over after the dance, but at her mother's house instead. The father was a bit confused, feeling left out. He asked his daughter what was behind her decision to not take him up on his offer. A bit reluctant, the daughter later shared that her bio mom had stated:

> *"Why would you want to go over to your dad's house after the dance when you can have your friends over here to watch a movie on **our** new 52-inch TV?"*

This is a form of manipulation. The daughter in this case may not even see that point. The parent/child bond is very strong! We shared with

the couple who felt a bit overlooked and ignored to take it in stride and default to understanding teenage girls. Often "home" tends to be where the mom lives.

As we have observed over the last several years, our kids tend to gravitate to the "mother hen's" nest. Dads, don't be dejected here. It just seems stepfamilies with whom we talk to tend to see more time spent at mom's house. It is home for most. Pick your battles carefully and do your best to not alienate your kids. As they grow older, I (Gil) have to keep reminding myself how I related with my parents to retain perspective. At their age, being connected to my parents and directly with my dad was not even on my radar. So to expect teens or older kids to fit my ideal is a struggle at times but beyond control. When they do interact with me it is respectful and that is much to be thankful for.

Moving from "no strings" attached as an illustration, now let's talk about buckets. This concept came to us by reading Elizabeth Einstein's *Strengthening Your Stepfamily.*[4] The "bucket" represents the emotional state of the children's well-being as they travel to and from the mother and father's home, respectfully. They carry some favorite belonging that brings security or a special game they can enjoy. But the bucket can become extremely heavy, depending on what is getting said to the child by one parent about the other.

Over time, the bucket can really begin to fill up with negative thoughts and emotions. Insinuations weigh heavy upon the child, whether they know it or not. And depending on the child's ability or inability to cope, the bucket can weigh them down even more. The child may not know how to unload the "rocks" that are building up in his/her bucket. Their well-being can become downcast or even defeated because they don't know how to tell their parents to stop such actions. See it from their point of view for a moment. The child may have a great relationship with the other bio parent and is excited to see them. Because you, the other parent, have harbored resentments or jealousy is no reason to dump that on the child before or after they get to see their other parent.

Rocks in your kids' buckets are more or less off-the-cuff remarks that you make as digs against your ex-spouse to your kids. Did you forget

a

ab

abab

ab

ababab

ba

ab

abab

ababab

abab

abab

ab

ababab

ab

that these offenses—real or perceived— at your end are between you and the ex? Your kid has nothing to do with the whole predicament. So why then are you dumping rocks or burdens in your kid's bucket that damage his/her well being? I (Gil) am coming down hard on this issue because this was something I did myself. When I realized what I was doing, I wept. Each time I share this concept I get choked up. I still recall the look in my daughter's eyes or see the expression on my son's face as a result of some of the offhanded remarks I made.

Listen as I describe to you what this sounds like when a rock has been dropped into your kid's bucket. Imagine your child standing in the doorway getting ready to be picked up by the other bio parent for visitation time. (That fact in itself should rock your world with pain enough for the child.) Picture them standing there with a five-gallon galvanized bucket. There may be a couple of small pebbles in there, plus a toy of some sort. It's a fairly easy load. They are lighthearted and prepared to head out the door.

While waiting, you make some remarks that sound like this:

> "Is your dad still going out with that gal?" (Tone is, of course, accusatorial.)

Listen, did you hear the rock? Or maybe you say…

> "Have your mom buy those shoes for you. I give her support money."

BAM goes a rock at the bottom of the metal bucket. Or, a rock could be dropped in this fashion…

> "Why do I always have to drive you back to your dad's?"

THUD as one rock cracks on top of another already in the bucket. Can you just see the countenance in your child change?

Disloyalty

If you did not hear the rocks collide with the bottom of the metal buckets, allow me to crank up the volume. When the mom said, "Is

ab

abab

abab

ab

ababab

ab

abab

abab

ab

ababab

ab

abab

abab

ab

ababab

ab

abab

abab

ab

ababab

ab

abab

abab

ab

ababab

ab

abab

abab

ab

ababab

RESTORED & Remarried

that these offenses—real or perceived— at your end are between you and the ex? Your kid has nothing to do with the whole predicament. So why then are you dumping rocks or burdens in your kid's bucket that damage his/her well being? I (Gil) am coming down hard on this issue because this was something I did myself. When I realized what I was doing, I wept. Each time I share this concept I get choked up. I still recall the look in my daughter's eyes or see the expression on my son's face as a result of some of the offhanded remarks I made.

Listen as I describe to you what this sounds like when a rock has been dropped into your kid's bucket. Imagine your child standing in the doorway getting ready to be picked up by the other bio parent for visitation time. (That fact in itself should rock your world with pain enough for the child.) Picture them standing there with a five-gallon galvanized bucket. There may be a couple of small pebbles in there, plus a toy of some sort. It's a fairly easy load. They are lighthearted and prepared to head out the door.

While waiting, you make some remarks that sound like this:

> "Is your dad still going out with that gal?" (Tone is, of course, accusatorial.)

Listen, did you hear the rock? Or maybe you say…

> "Have your mom buy those shoes for you. I give her support money."

BAM goes a rock at the bottom of the metal bucket. Or, a rock could be dropped in this fashion…

> "Why do I always have to drive you back to your dad's?"

THUD as one rock cracks on top of another already in the bucket. Can you just see the countenance in your child change?

Disloyalty

If you did not hear the rocks collide with the bottom of the metal buckets, allow me to crank up the volume. When the mom said, "Is

your dad still going out with that gal?" this is asking the child to be disloyal to his/her father with information they may not know. Or, they are aware that it would hurt you if they shared. If that describes something you've said, realize a five-pound rock is being toted around in your kid's bucket that you put there! Think of that load carried over time.

Money

Next, when you said, "Have your mom buy those shoes for you. I give her support money," realize the message this ten-pound rock is giving your child. They may interpret your comment to be about them—that they are not worth your money. How would you like to carry that around for a while?

Time

Lastly, while you are transporting your child, "Why do I always have to drive you back to your dad's?" Maybe the agreement in the parenting plan was to trade off the transporting chore, but the point that comes across to the child is they are a burden and not worth your time or seeing to their safety.

Don't slam the bio parent when the children are present! Frankly, it does nothing to improve the ex's behavior, even if they are a schmuck. The disrespect that it breeds will have a long-term affect on the child's ability to relate in a healthy manner for the long haul. If you've dropped a rock in your kid's bucket, ask for forgiveness. Show them you desire to lighten their load just by making known you understand what you've done. Hopefully, they will realize you're aware of their plight. This can restore them, as well and improve their well-being. Children want to be loved and to love their parents. Heaping burdens on that desire or emptying their buckets, which is more loving?

The parent team mentality of the marriage and getting behind your wall for protection only benefits the kids, even if the protection is *from* the kids! Your kids will find security in their home when they see that your marriage is secure. No matter how your relationship is with your ex or your spouse's ex, the key is to keep the kids' welfare in the forefront of the co-parenting relationship.

End of Chapter Questions

1. Dads: What are you doing to help your kids and stepkids grow spiritually?

   _____

   _____

   _____

2. Moms: What are you doing to help your kids and stepkids grow spiritually?

   _____

   _____

   _____

3. What kind of co-parenting relationship do you have with your ex? Does it need to be adjusted for the sake of the kids? Remember, you can only adjust your part unless you have a relationship with the ex that allows you to talk about this and maybe share this information.

_____

_____

_____

4. Name three places in which you may need to go back to and do some cutting and cauterizing. Plan a time to "take care of business," by yourself if needed.

_____

_____

_____

5. How in tune are you with the betrayal factor? If you have been hurt or over-reacted in the past, can you have an honest conversation with the child and let them know it's OK; to encourage them to love their bio parent.

_____

_____

_____

6. Do you have any "strings" you need to cut?

_____

_____

_____

7. What may have been a rock that you put in your kid's bucket? Once identified, explain the "rocks in the bucket concept" to your kids and ask for forgiveness.

_____

_____

_____

8. Have you added any new words/terms to your wall lately? Take some time to create a new one!

_____

_____

_____

Action Item:

Go somewhere or do something you have never done, to build new history. Be intentional with a theme: adventurous, silly, educating…get the idea?

> *"The most important thing a father can do for his*
>
> *children is to love their mother."*
>
> **—Theodore Hesburgh**

Chapter 7

Two Countries and an Elephant

Chapter 7

Two Countries & an Elephant

Why Parents Get Gray Hair

A father passing by his son's bedroom was astonished to see the bed nicely made up and everything neat and tidy. Then he saw an envelope propped up prominently on the pillow. It was addressed, "Dad." With the worst premonition, he opened the envelope and read the letter with trembling hands:

> *Dear Dad, it is with great regret and sorrow that I'm writing you. I had to elope with my new girlfriend because I wanted to avoid a scene with you and Mom. I've been finding real passion with Joan and she is so nice. I knew you would not approve of her because of all her piercing, tattoos, her tight motorcycle clothes and because she is so*

much older than I am. But it's not only the passion, Dad. She's pregnant. Joan says that we are going to be very happy. She owns a trailer in the woods and has a stack of firewood, enough for the whole winter. We share a dream of having many more children. Joan has opened my eyes to the fact that marijuana doesn't really hurt anyone. We'll be growing it and trading it with the other people in the commune for all the cocaine and ecstasy we want. In the meantime, we'll pray that science will find a cure for AIDS so Joan can get better. She sure deserves it.

Don't worry, Dad. I'm 15-years-old now and I know how to take care of myself. Someday, I'm sure we'll be back to visit so you can get to know your grandchildren.

Your son, Chad (and SCOTTIE & MAX)

P.S. Dad, none of the above is true. I'm over at Tommy's house. I just wanted to remind you that there are worse things in life than the report card that's in my desk drawer.

I love you! Call when it is safe for me to come home.

Pick a favorite country to which you like to travel. Go ahead, pick a country. Maybe it's Canada, Scotland, or Italy. Now choose a country that would be last on your list. For instance, Iceland (because of the cold climate), or a small island country like Bora Bora (because it is deserted and you are stranded). How about a foreign country that you'd not want to live in because personal freedoms are limited? OK, do have them chosen? Ask yourself this question next, "How would you survive or fare having to travel between those two chosen countries on a regular basis?"

Dual citizenship, I've heard, can be a great benefit to a person, provided that the society and cultures are similar. Knowing the behavior or social order of how to conduct oneself, may take a while to get used to. But once you master each way of lfe, living in two countries could be tolerable, and even enjoyable.

Enjoyable vs. intolerable all depends on the host you live with in each country. Teaching you how to shift between the two locales would be a great benefit. But what if one of your hosts had a crummy attitude or had a hard time expressing themselves? Disadvantages may cause you to stumble because you can't comprehend the language very well, or you misinterpret terms and concepts between the two nations.

Let's say this traveling between the two countries is a pattern that you learn to navigate pretty well until one country declares war on the other. Worse yet, the war is raging and you are given no say in your travel itinerary. You are still required to make the trips to and fro. It is never known when one country will lob a bomb at the other, and you sometimes find carnage of some sort.

The changeover becomes much like a POW swap back in the '50s and '60s—shuffled across the Iron Curtain between East Berlin and West Berlin. The whole arrangement blows your mind, yet somehow you endure. Concern for your personal safety is not in question because the hosts from both countries really like you. As a matter of fact, they give you special treatment at times to gain your favor or loyalty. After learning their tactics, an advantage falls your way as you learn how to manipulate the situation and play one off the other, that is until they figure out what you are up to.

The situation your kids now face as a result of your divorce is somewhat similar. They are traveling between two different nations. They are dual citizens of two different lands. They do their best to keep their wits about them to be sure their conduct is pleasing in both environments. Maybe they get weary of trying and some just give up. They may rebel against both systems and dig into a cave to hide until the war is over.

What if those countries at war are your parents and you are trying to create a peace treaty between them? If nobody is coming to the negotiating table and you are asked to join one side or the other, then what? The switch between the two would then indeed start to feel like a POW swap!

Here is what one of our kids shared (age nineteen when we got married, twenty-six now).

> "I can't help but give my two cents (as you have come to

know about me) on children moving between house to house of divorcees. I can't even imagine what it is like. I envy my siblings and stepsiblings for enduring the complete polar shifts from one house to the other. I can only envision it as spending a winter in Antarctica and being forced to take an hour plane trip to the Congo and being told that you have to acclimate yourself or be decapitated (sorry, I have a sick sense of humor). But seriously, I don't think kids should have to endure this punishment on behalf of the parents' mistakes."

We knew for a fact that our kids were dealing with lifestyles and belief systems in the other home that were far different than ours. Not that we were at war or that overt battle lines were visible; but for the sake of discussion, we could safely say the atmosphere was close to a cold war. Discussions or attitudes that were carried between the two homes were noticeable and our children's coping skills were being taxed above and beyond the call of duty.

> *Is it true, is it necessary, and most of all—is it loving?*

Depending upon the child, they would bring back with them open, hard-hitting questions or stonewall silence. We wondered in some instances how to love them and nurture their well-being without seeming like we were prying into the other home's business. Don't forget about the dumping of rocks into the child's bucket. It is nearly impossible to avoid such things in such charged circumstances.

So, you say then, "What am I supposed to do?"

Pray! No, I am not kidding, pray! Be silent and ask God for wisdom.

Keep your mouth shut until you get the answer for that specific incident. Then let this be your rule of discourse with what you have to say:

Is it true, is it necessary, and most of all—is it loving?

While the changing of homes takes place, keep in mind a couple of moorings of stability for the child:

Give the child time to adjust when he/she comes back from the other home. The amount of time can vary depending on the kid. For some it may be hours and others it can be a couple of days. Give them space or wrap your arms around them and hold them. Ask them what they want or need. You will be surprised what you'll learn and it helps them express their hearts.

Give the kid a heads-up as to what has been going on in your home. Share activities or events that have taken place, or what they can expect coming up in your home while they are there. Offer them a briefing, if you'd like to think of it that way, so they are not coming into the home cold with no idea what everyone has been up to. Don't forget to give them an idea of the role they play in your home on a daily basis.

Since this transfer of children will be a part of their life and yours from this point forward, blended families have to have a plan to keep the peace as best as possible. As they grow older, their choice to visit your home or not will be founded on whether they're feeling welcomed. You, as the parents, may think you have a welcoming, warm home to your kids/stepkids. They may be coming in with a different set of lenses—a different view. You may be doing all the "right things" and they see it as polar opposite. It's frustrating, for sure! But remember, we're not the ones dealing with constant change. That is our kid's job. Have the attitude that you're not going anywhere, you're in this for the long haul. And most of all, love on them the best you can.

Life goes on. How you handle the here and now will affect the future. Anticipate pain and rejection even if you think you did a good job with this facet of your kid's upbringing in the midst of the blended family.

Stay with the rules that fit your lifestyle. Allow them to be the house

rules. Be considerate of the fact that the kid will learn to navigate the terrain far better while being loved, accepted, and as age appropriation gives way, the freedom to choose how they will love you in return.

Lastly, relax! They want to love you. Blood is blood and nobody can take your kid's love from you. Even in the perfect intact family, parents still get rejected. Keep in mind that eventually if love is given and taken in a healthy manner, it will win the day. Remember…you are not going anywhere. Learning to love Those People takes time—especially if you don't even know them as you begin the expedition of your blended family.

One and Ones with the Folks

Within the first month of our new adventure together, it was becoming apparent that some kids were adjusting easier than others. Everyone was being cordial to each other, but there was something in the air. You could sense apprehension, anger, fear, sadness, and happiness. Gil and I decided to boldly go where no stepparent had gone before (at least that we knew of).

We invited each child in for a "meeting" with us. Gil would say this to his kids; I would say it to mine. This is how it was explained so they knew what they were walking into:

"We realize that you have had some adjusting to do with all the changes. You have done a wonderful job. We just want to give you a safe place to share how you really feel. How are things going for you? How can we support you better? There isn't anything you can say that is off-limits. We will not hold anything against you. We love you and care about your heart. We are not going anywhere. The only thing we ask is that you be as honest as you possibly can. This is just a starting place for an ongoing conversation."

There were tears, awkward silence, laughter, and hugs. We all had a say in how we were feeling about our new life circumstances and acknowledged that some were still grieving the loss of their previous family. We also shared how we felt about each other. I think it really helped for the kids to hear where we were coming from too. As the

stepparent I (Brenda) was a little apprehensive and was trying to be so careful not to hurt my stepkids' feelings! It was really important to me that they felt at home. Not only was this where their father resided, but we were trying to establish a safe place for them. By sharing that with them, I had hoped that they appreciated my effort, even if I was missing the mark! At least they knew my intentions were for their best interest.

It was an incredible bonding experience for us. We also learned some things. The easiest way to do this is to start with the most talkative kid! The first meeting for the parent/stepparent can be just as scary as for the kids! We started with the easiest kids and worked our way to the hardest. Our confidence was built and we felt more relaxed to communicate better with the child who may have needed some extra encouragement.

After each conversation, we always ended in prayer—acknowledging that the Lord was a part of our time together. It brought strength to our relationships, and reminded us of the most important factor—the Lord. We let the kids know all the time that we are praying for them. And we do! By laying this foundation with our kids, it made future conversations or meeting times easier and more comfortable. Our kids all knew that if they needed to talk, we were there for them…all of them!

Here is what one of our kids shared (age fifteen when we got married, twenty one now):

> *"I felt surprised and a little intimidated at first when I sat down alone in a room with Gil, but began to open up as he made his best effort to shoot straight with me about his intentions with my mom and his interest in my own life. I felt like Gil had paved a clear foundation for my relationship and I could trust him."*

We hesitate to even use the word "meetings" in the previous interactions. That sounds rather cold and unemotional. The intimate interactions that happened, whether there were tears or laughter involved, brought us closer. They helped us understand one another and get our arms around this whole new living arrangement called a stepfamily. Are

we walking arm and arm into the sunset, everyone together? In some moments, yes, in some moments, no. We were daring enough to take the step toward our kids, all of them, to show them we care and that we were making an effort for their heart.

Here is what another one of our kids shared (age sixteen when we got married, twenty-two now):

> "I recall the 'meeting,' so the parents called it. I thought of it more as an interference with my video games. At that age I had many mixed emotions and hormones exploding through my mind. It's hard to recall how I approached the conversation I had with my father and stepmother that morning. However, I will never forget the love and patience they showed to us kids as our families came together. I think it's important with any blended family to show patience and grace, as long as your stepbrother isn't stealing your socks. Time is also a key factor in my opinion. We learn to love and grow with each other more as time goes on, along with the experiences we share with one another."

A Saturday to Remember

Those People were in rare form one Saturday morning, about six months after we had been married. The laundry basket caravan had been going on for a while. (Laundry basket caravan was how our kids would travel between the two houses.) Territorialism had become an issue that was creating tension in our happy home. The "honeymooners" were adjusting and had only encountered a couple of bumps thus far. But the strain of the new people living with us, from my (Gil) stepson's perspective, and the new environment I was requiring my bio kids to travel through was novel, fun, and then not so pleasant. Honestly, a couple of my kids to this day still find it hard to call this home

By ten o'clock that Saturday morning you could sense the apprehension and tension coming from upstairs. Three teenagers and two preteens, you can image the scraggly appearance that was displayed by the five of them. Brenda, I recall, was out that morning for coffee with a girlfriend. I was left alone to feed and face Those People. Nothing was

planned to tackle these issues, let alone to encounter it by myself, but I felt it was my position to step forward and lead. I went to my room and prayed for wisdom. I came out and called for a family meeting. Five against one!

Starting with the issue of our home and the world they contended with daily at school, safety was my chief concern for all of the kids. Safety in that when they entered the doors of our home, they could let their guard down and know that they could be themselves. Central to the talk was that home was to be a safety zone for all of them. Instruction was given to set a precedent. I was aware of the situation and I was calling for a ceasefire.

Five against one!

I acknowledged that my stepsons were dealing with major adjustments. After they had grown used to being in a single mom household, they now had two new stepsiblings and a stepfather. Sure, they could have seen it as an invasion of their space, as age and pecking order had to be sorted out. A major remodeling project had taken place in less than four months. And now the reality of life change again was in their face.

As I write about this time in our family, I wonder what it would have been like if my two oldest sons had been part of the equation. My second oldest son has stayed with us only a handful of times and my oldest son never has. I saw this at the time as their choice to not engage with the new reality of their father's life. As time has marched on and honest conversations have taken place with them, their attitudes have come around to accept what is now family. Brenda and I continue to stay with the "we're not going anywhere" mentality.

That Saturday morning continued with more direct comments by me to diffuse the tension rocking the new family structure. Here's what I

did. I gave an outline of the family structure as lovingly as possible. My goal was to help clear the air. First, I looked at my two kids who were living with us part-time and made the point that Brenda was not their mother, but she was my wife. She was not there to take their mother's place but was to be respected as my wife. She loved and accepted them for who they were. She was the mother at this home and could be trusted.

Next, I looked at my new sons with a bit of trepidation. (Even then I did not want to overstep my authority.) I had chosen to lead, so I went for it by saying that I was not their father but that I was their mother's husband. I respected, loved, and was committed to their mom. I was not replacing their father, but was now the father of this house and it was my place to keep the peace for all who live here. From there, it was all mystery and a fog. Here is a bit of their story to finish out this section...

Here is what one of our kids shared (age fifteen when we got married, twenty-one now):

> *"I felt that these meetings really helped me understand how my new family was going to operate because I would better understand how my mom was going to respond to my stepsiblings. If we didn't come to a community understanding of which parent played which role in our lives, I think things would have remained awkward for years. I am so thankful my parents sat down and did this."*

Pink Elephant

John and his stepson Josh were really struggling in their relationship. John noticed that every time Josh came for the weekend, he gave John the silent treatment. John tried to connect with Josh at many different levels. He would take him out to play video games, they would go to the batting cages and, of course, they would always stop at Josh's favorite store to get a scoop of cookie dough ice cream. John did not know how else to connect with this young man. It was as if when John tried to engage, the hand went in front of his face as if to say, "John, don't go there, don't talk to me." This was an ongoing challenge for John.

That, my friends, is when it is time to bring out the pink elephant!

When we encountered scenarios like the one just described, it was termed "pink elephant time." This time could be with one child or with the whole family. We would bring everyone together and bring "it" out. A friend gave us this incredible stuffed pink elephant. He's about one foot by two feet tall. When it was "meeting" time, we would bring the animal out. The kids all knew what it meant. We were going to talk about something that was being neglected—the pink elephant in the room that no one wanted to talk about. It had been there awhile (no short accounts here!) and was starting to stink up the place.

This was our way to say, "We are not going to operate like this any more. It's time to talk about what's really going on…it's time to clear the air."

Trust and honesty were put to the test. Having a place to share how we were feeling about what was going on had to happen. Once you become "real," you can get to the root of the problem. A lot of the time someone has just been misunderstood. It's amazing what happens when we all slow down long enough, look each other in the eye, and listen!

It is so important to have these conversations. Isn't it just like the "enemy" to attack and divide our families? If he can get a foothold in our family relationships, he can then isolate members, thus taking us out one by one. Unresolved issues affect the whole family and weaken the ties we have to each other. Stepfamily ties can be fragile to begin with. The demise of another family is the goal of this slimy monster and we need to be aware of what is really going on in the spiritual realms.

A fresh clean spring scent fills the room once the pink elephant has been put to rest. Can it be uncomfortable to have these discussions? Sometimes. Do they need to happen? Absolutely.

Stepparents, be the adult. Be brave. Fight for your kids' hearts. Fight for the legacy of your family! Make sure you acknowledge the progress made after the "pink elephant time." Then kids won't be apprehensive to have short accounts!

Home vs. House

I (Brenda) have become very sensitive to language in our home. I'm not talking about the bad words or swear words specifically. Let me give you an example. When one of my stepkids says they are coming home (and they mean our house), in my mind I do a victory dance! I see it as a "win." It may not seem like much to you, but I want my stepkids to think of our home as their home.

As Gil stated earlier, home is usually where Mom lives. But I want my stepkids to feel that they have two homes; not Mom's *home* and Dad's *house*. The connotation of home is warm and inviting and safe…or it should be. The goal is that our stepkids would feel that way about both homes. I want my kids to feel their dad's house is their home too.

Our kids travel between two "countries." If your ex's country does not hold the same values as yours, here are a few tips:

> *I do a victory dance!*

- Stand firm and be consistent with where you "live." If you are a Christ-follower and the other parent is not, what a great opportunity to show His love. It's important to speak truth without slamming the other parent. And because loyalties can run deep, be open and not judgmental to what your child shares. If they resonate more with the other parent, that can hurt, especially if things don't line up with your values. Always default to love. Living our consistent relationship with Christ will win in the end. And it never hurts to pray!

- Show a strong Parent Team. Healthy parenting puts boundaries in place for kids. Most kids will challenge the boundaries, and that's OK. If they know that you two have talked and show a united front, they will be less likely to play

you against each other. Do not forget to get behind your wall in these situations!

- Model a healthy marriage. Do you want your kids to have the marriage that was like your previous one? Here is an incredible gift you can give all your kids right now—a glimpse into a loving, committed, selfless marriage that is based on trust and honesty.

The Law of the Land

Different rules in each home will cause conflict, not only for you but also for the kid. It's important to have clearly explained expectations so everyone is on the same page. The rules in this home are just that, the rules /guidelines in *this* home:

- Homework before or after dinner?

- OK to eat with the TV on?

- Who does the dishes?

- Make your lunch or buy it at school?

We suggest lots of flexibility here. If one child does better doing homework after dinner rather than before, that's fine. If a stepsibling has to do their homework right after school, you may find an argument brewing over "fairness." An open discussion about that is important, making sure everyone knows why they may not be doing the same things at the same time (i.e. homework). What's best for each child?

If the other home does not have a curfew and your home does, you know that will be thrown in your face. Without disrespecting the other home, clearly lay out your expectations in THIS home. And be sure to tell them why. Even though the kids may not agree with your "rules," if it is for their safety and to help build their character, stand firm.

When kids have duties in your home, they will feel more a part of the family. We're not saying every time they come over they have a Cinderella complex and spend all their time cleaning. You guys (the

parents) need to decide which hills are worth dying upon.

Yes, kids need to learn responsibility. But don't forget where they are emotionally, especially early on. Traveling between two houses is not only tough emotionally, but logistically too. Do they have their toothbrush, enough pairs of underwear, their special curling iron or favorite video game? It's a good idea to keep some of the staples at your home all the time so they don't have to worry about them. Spending a little to have things in place will save you worlds of expended emotional energy in the future.

We tried to keep each child's schedule the same. It was probably more work for us in the long run, but that is OK. Keeping things as normal as possible helps add stability to both the kids and the family. Remember, they did not ask for any of this!

Just like we shared in Chapter 4, we need to S.U.R.F. (S= servanthood; U= unity; R= relationship; F= flexibility) in our family as well as our marriage. When the tsunamis of kid issues start hitting, ask your spouse, "How's the SURFing?" And then be sure to laugh (or at least smile).

Traditions and Holidays

Bringing two families together can be quite interesting, especially around the holidays. These times of year somehow intensify emotions and relationships that may already be on edge. But that can happen even in nuclear families. Navigating the celebration waters throughout the year can feel like fighting against a strong current or gliding on a lake of glass. To keep you on the "gliding on a lake of glass" scenario, you have to look at your attitude. Think of it as a way to use your creative juices to start new memories or family history. And during the birthing of this new family history there may be birthing pains that, in the long run, will be totally worth it. Laughter is key.

It was our first Christmas together with five of our kids at home. We were off to hunt for the perfect Christmas tree. We piled into two cars and made the trek to our local forest. Well, really it was a tree farm, but living in the Northwest the rest of the world thinks we go to the forest

through winding roads and snow-covered mountains, climbing to the sky, to find our Christmas tree. Might as well perpetuate the idea.

I (Brenda) was ready. I had hot chocolate ready in thermoses, tons of marshmallows, and, of course, whipping cream. On the way we talked about funny Christmas tree stories from our past and how big the trees were that were cut, each kid trying to outdo the other. We were ready to "make history" for our new family.

We hit the farm running to see who would find the best tree first. Then the "discussion" occurred, the first of many concerning this Christmas tree tradition.

"Well, we've always gotten Douglas firs," one kid piped up.

"Well, since I was a kid we had nobles."

"I like space between the branches so the ornaments will fit."

"Ours was usually at least eight feet tall."

On and on this conversation went as voices were raised and attitudes appeared. Luckily, before we had an all-out brawl on the Christmas tree farm, we came to a compromise that everyone could live with. Driving away with our "kill" on the top of our car, everyone was satisfied with our choice. Phew. OK, that was "fun," Gil and I said to each other. Little did we know what was around the next bend.

It took us all of about thirty minutes to get home. As we unloaded the tree into the family room everyone helped position it. "A little to the left, a little to the right. OK, good." I had the ornaments out and ready to put on the tree. Because Gil didn't have any of his own ornaments, Kara (Gil's daughter) and I had gone out previously to buy some new ornaments for our family. I didn't want the whole tree only covered in my old ornaments. As we were ready to start the traditional decorating of the tree, I had to do what I had ALWAYS done! Put Amy Grant's Christmas CD on. That was tradition!

As the first couple of ornaments were placed on the tree, another "discussion" occurred.

"This is the way we hang the ornaments."

"Don't throw the tinsel, you place it."

"The lights are tucked back into the tree more."

"The lights need to be out front so you can see them."

On and on this conversation went as voices were raised and attitudes appeared once again. *Gee, this is sounding strangely familiar*, I thought, *in a sick-to-my-stomach sort of way.*

"I have an idea," Gil said. "Let's draw an imaginary line down the center of the tree. You guys decorate it the way you want on this side, you guys decorate it the way you want on that side."

That suggestion seemed to quiet the natives. We had a very eclectic tree but it was wonderful. All was going well until…the question. It was the mother of all questions. Kyle, Gil's son, said, "Why do we have to listen to Amy Grant? That's stupid." Ahh, stab me in the heart, will ya? Don't you know it is tradition to play Amy Grant as we decorate the Christmas tree? Don't you know all the happy memories associated with listening to this at this very moment? Don't you have any idea how much Amy Grant's music influenced me and my walk with the Lord? Don't you…. On and on I went in my mind as I went over and turned the music off.

No, Kyle didn't know all that was behind that silly little cassette. How could he? He had not been with me the last fifteen years as I had listened to this music. He didn't have the history with me to appreciate it. He spoke innocently, and just how he felt. I know he didn't say that to hurt me or make me mad. I don't remember if I put on other music or if we continued in silence. I don't think the kids even noticed. I do regret how I handled it though. What a great opportunity I missed to share with Kyle a little about myself and how Amy's music had ministered to me through the years. Lesson learned.

Now when we decorate the tree, it's a group effort. And it doesn't look half bad! Since the first Christmas, I have bought ornaments for each kid who is living in the house at the time. It has been such a blessing every year when we pull them out and see the date of when they were

first hung on our tree; it's almost like a badge of honor that our family is growing together and building history.

Traditions. It's good to keep some old ones going. But what new traditions have you started in your family? Is it a weekly movie night or a Sunday dinner? Amy Marsh and her new family started the No Hands Dinner tradition. When Amy would serve this dinner the only rule was "No Hands!"

"What we serve depends on whatever is being cooked. But it is a lot funnier if it is harder to eat with no silverware. Pancakes have been by far the hardest. Spaghetti was really easy though. This is what we do: I cook dinner and let the kids know it's a no-hands night. We get the table all set, food dished, drinks served, and pray.

"From prayer on, you are not allowed to use your hands in any way, shape, or form. Tie your hair up and dig in. It is best to get cups that have a lip on them so they are easier to grab with your teeth (straws are cheating). If it is something like potatoes you get the potato ready, then the silverware is gone. Pancakes, you put the butter and syrup on but no cutting it up.

"To help build any family, I believe you need laughter and you have to be open. By doing a no-hands dinner, we showed the kids that we all can have fun and laugh together. It builds memories. The kids can still tell you all the different meals we have eaten. We had to trust one another a bit because we are all going to be looking very messy and you have to learn to loosen up and let go of the fear of being made fun of because we are all doing it together. Expect messes though. Spilled drinks, food on the table, etc. We have even had to tie up our hands because it was so hard one time."

What a riot! Talk about building history! How daring are you?

Traditions and holidays. These can be treacherous waters but can be conquered and become a starting point for history! And, if an idea you come up with totally bombs, no fear; it'll be recalled over and over with a lot of laughter and "I can't believe you made us do that" comments that only bring more bonding. As we've said over and over, laughter is key.

Discipline

While attending a marriage and family conference in Scottsdale, Arizona, a couple of years ago, one of the break-out sessions was conducted by Moe and Paige Becnel of Baton Rouge, Louisiana. During the session, which was specific to stepfamily dynamics and discipline of young children, one of the attendees was floored to learn that they had been counseling stepfamilies—namely stepfathers—completely wrong!

This counselor had been directing the stepfathers to lay down the law within the family and require that things be done a specific way. Needless to say, his counseling sessions were not having the desired effect as the stepfamily couples would be back with the same problems time and time again. Admittedly, he confessed that even intact families (not having been through a divorce) where the mother and father were on the same page in agreement encountered difficulties with this line of discipline and parenting.

Of course, rules are rules. Therefore, relationships that were directly with biological parents would logically give parents a bit more leverage in their approach. Being loving and firm is to be respected regardless of whether you are a father or stepfather; the roles are very similar but worlds apart. The same holds true for mothers and stepmothers with their roles requiring the respect and obedience of the children. Idealistic for sure—stepmothers usually get a bad wrap, some deservedly.

During the session, the counselor began to understand that approaching house rules and discipline in the stepfamily scenario is a completely different animal. Without relationships being established first, the stepparent exerting his/her perceived authority was getting no traction. Instead, it produced disastrous family conflicts. Worse yet, it was creating problems in the marriage as well as issues with the children. Each parent was getting defensive of his/her own child. This can be a big time dividing point for the couple. And your wall can suffer as a result.

One couple shares the following experience:

"After being married for a few months, Rob was taking the initiative to discipline my two kids. In some situations I felt he really mishandled

the situations. He was being unrealistic with his expectations of my kids. Pride and insecurity made me question how safe I was to share with him, and kept me from letting him know how hurt I was. The momma bear in me came out. Being protective of my kids was my job.

Stepmothers usually get a bad wrap.

"I found myself unconscientiously looking for ways to get even with his kids. This was not a good situation. Then, of course, he became defensive of how I was disciplining his kids. It finally got to the point that we had to get our pink elephant out. Behind closed doors, we both agreed it was time to be honest. This was really hard. I shared with Rob that I felt he was moving too fast and too soon with correcting my kids. I felt he needed to slow down and focus on building a relationship with them. If he was having a problem with something they were doing, I would like him to come to me first. I said I would do the same with his kids.

"We both came into this conversation with our defenses up. But once we realized we both wanted what was best for each of our kids, we were back on track to working as a team."

Once that issue got resolved and the parents began to keep a position of unity, they could see some progress. Results were a peaceful home rather than disharmony by working within the framework of the child's established respect and learned parental authority.

At last, the counselor began to understand the more effective approach was to allow biological parents to dish out the discipline first, rather than laying down rules like you had always been there. Once understanding

and trust is built, a stepparent can step in with more of a stern manner. In some circumstances that position of parental authority may never be exactly the same as it would be with your own children.

Stepparents must respect the parental bond between the child(ren) and the bio parent. Once again, as the stepparent, let the stepchild set the pace of your relationship. Trying to rush the process to establish authority in the home is not the question. You are the adult, you need to be respected. But expect it to be questioned, pushed, tried, and challenged! If you recall the "crockpot method," you may be refreshed in your thinking that this stepfamily expedition will take time—lots of time. You also need to be flexible while keeping harmony and influence.

In my (Gil's) situation, I was very patient with my stepguys, working hard to earn their respect. That took time. And I had to bite my lip quite frequently in how they interacted with my wife (their mother). There was tension in how my kids reacted to this style of family life.

Then the reverse was true for Brenda and my kids. The issue of discipline or metering out correction often would be deferred until the matter could be discussed between us. Then the appropriate actions would be dealt out depending on whose kid it was—Brenda with her sons and me with my kids.

Here is what another one of our kids shared (age twelve when we got married, eighteen now):

> "Living in a stepfamily was rough in the beginning. It takes a lot of patience, especially on the parent's side. I'm lucky to have Gil as a stepdad because he waited for me to accept him for about two or three years. I'm sure it wasn't easy for him, but he waited for me and it paid off.
>
> "The first year is always rough. Everyone has their own tradition of doing things and that's why it's always good to make completely new traditions. The biggest thing was in the first year or two. My mom punished me most of the time. Gil would obviously have his say in it, but I needed that space, and he gave it to me. Overall it takes perseverance

to keep the stepfamily going. But it's very possible. So if anybody is ever thinking about divorce because they think their families won't ever blend, they have got to push through. Marriage vows should not just be thrown out the window because it's hard."

Babysitter Method

How does the transfer of power from the bio parent to the stepparent work? The babysitter technique of transferring authority to your new spouse is the proven way to do this. Let's say you, the bio parent, need to run some errands, leaving the stepparent home alone with your kids. Here's a suggestion of what you can do to build "step-authority." Whether they are five or fifteen years old, get eye contact with your child. Once you see they are listening to you and acknowledge that you are not leaving, you make it very clear who is in charge—the stepparent.

In much the same way as a "babysitter" is given the mantle of authority when the parents are out, a five-year-old will understand this. The transfer is far more challenging with tweeners and teenagers because they think they know the rules and they think they make the rules.

> *Lower your expectations with the older kids, you will be more in touch with reality!*

Since the new stepparent in those first few years is establishing all the rights of a biological parent, the rights can be far more effectively conveyed by the babysitter method. In a way you are stating the obvious,

but it is better understood by the kids if you take the extra steps to communicate the position of the stepparent. Keep expectations very clear. Also let the kids know that the stepparent will let you know how everything went, just like a babysitter would.

Of course, we realize that acceptance can take longer—or shorter—depending on the age of the children involved. A younger child is far more influenced by a parental figure than an adolescent or teen who is trying out his/her independent wings, so to speak. Remember the equation of age acceptance? Take the age of the child at the time of the remarriage, multiply by two, and you'll get the general time it takes to find some level of loving acceptance. You don't necessarily have to be in love with your stepchild like the bio parent, but some respect and healthy human affection would be a nice goal. Hence, the younger the child, the quicker that could happen. The older they are, the more set and loyal they may be. Acceptance, let alone a voice of authority, will take longer. If you lower your expectations with the older kids, you will be more in touch with reality!

One illustration at that same marriage and family conference was role-played by another couple whose focus was stepparenting. Gordon and Carri Taylor, from *Dynamic Stepfamilies,*[1] had a great age-specific, situational, real-life drama of how to deal with Susie when she was five, and then later when she was sixteen.

Susie is the daughter of Mary. Joe had been Susie's stepdad for three months. One day, Susie is caught by Joe with her hand in the cookie jar! Susie was told to stay out of the cookie jar. Joe is a gentle guy but cookies are serious business and stealing is out of the question for this five-year-old girl. He wants to teach Susie a lesson but he was fortunate to take in this role-play lesson. He doesn't blow up or shout or spank Susie while Mary, her mom, is out of the home. He takes his rightful role—makes Susie put the cookies back in the jar and sends her to her room till mommy gets home.

Mary arrives home to find Susie banished to her room for taking a cookie (which, as agreed upon by the couple, is against the rules). She and Joe are OK with his actions. So far so good, right? The couple talks through the situation and concludes that Susie will be on cookie rations for a week. Susie is called downstairs by her parents to listen to

her penalty.

When sweet little Susie arrives front and center she finds her mom and stepdad standing in the kitchen with the evidence in hand. Joe is behind his wife, off to the side, showing support but not taking the predominate role he could have taken much earlier. He allows Susie's mom to dole out the discipline. Mary says to Susie, "We have made a decision…." Mary includes Joe in the mix of the events and his role in the cookie rations to follow over the next week. Joe and Mary show a united front to Susie, and Mary makes it clear that Joe, the stepdad, will take a more active role next time. (We all know there will be a next time.)

As sure as rain will fall in the Northwest in November, Susie (in spite of her sweetness) did her fair share of cookie stealing over the years, not to mention various other infractions. Each time Joe and Mary went through the same steps fairly consistently. But what was unique was that each time they went through this routine of discipline, Joe would move more to the front and alongside Mary while the doling out of penalties were administered. When the time came, Joe and Mary would eventually be standing side by side and Joe would be the one doing the talking. Mary, in turn, takes on more of the support role. Time and respect had been built to give Joe, the stepdad, a voice in this young girl's life.

Unfortunately, at the wonderful age of sweet sixteen, Susie chooses badly one day and swipes $50 from Joe's piggy bank! Not that Susie was a thief by nature; she just could not pass up the money in her stepdad's piggy bank to go buy a new dress for the prom! When the money was discovered missing and the truth surfaced, Susie could not come up with any story to clear her name. Joe is one cool dude—as stepdads go—and he kept his cool in this very sizzling situation. Mary was very sad that her daughter would stoop so low. If she simply asked for the money or worked out a chore to earn the money, they would have gladly made it work out. Now, that not being the case, Susie knows punishment will be hefty. She waits for her mom and stepdad (whom she really does admire at this point) to immerge from their room with the sentence for her crime.

Joe and Mary bring the young criminal lovingly to the judgment hall—better known as the kitchen. Over time, Joe has gained the respect, authority, and relationship with Susie to speak into Susie's life. Although Mary is present and is showing support, she allows Joe to do the talking, as stern as it may be. Their unity is still demonstrated. (Now, we know that in a perfect world this might be the case. Only in a perfect world does the story end so positively. Only in a perfect world

> *W*e're not putting the marriage before the kids; it's the foundation FOR the kids.

does the stepdad execute all the plays exactly to a "T", but work with us here....)

If we as stepparents will take these long and tedious steps, they will pay off and be worth it in the long haul. Had the steps not been taken, the outcome for Susie at sixteen would have been way different. Just ask us! We did not get all this right with our own kids, but we sure did get a lot of practice with real situations that put this system to the test.

We share the next quote with the utmost respect for a dear friend of a friend who introduced this thought to us. As a concluding point, consider this...

>*Rules without relationship produce rebellion.*

>*Relationship without rules produces promiscuity.*

>*Rules and relationship produce effective parenting.*

What sacrifices will the marriage make to serve the kids? Even in nuclear families in the name of being "a good parent" we serve our kids at the

expense of our marriage, especially if the marriage isn't going well. It's so easy to hide behind our kids. This is when you need to retreat behind your wall and regroup! Don't let the kids come between you. This is a tough balancing act. We're not putting the marriage before the kids; it's the foundation FOR the kids.

Acronym Time!

We have encouraged you to create acronyms for your marriage and then add them as bricks to your wall. Now it's time to create a brick/wall for your family. This is a great way to get all your kids involved. Grab a couple of cartons of ice cream and go for it! The word is TEAM.

> ***TEAM***: *to yoke or join in a team; marked by devotion to teamwork rather than individual achievement; two or more draft animals harnessed to the same vehicle or implement.*
> **—Webster's Dictionary**

What does your family think of when they see the word TEAM? What words represent those thoughts? If you have younger kids who can't write yet, involve them by writing down their input. Here is what we came up with for our family's TEAM:

T   trust

E   enthusiasm

A   action

M   maturity

You can create other words that represent foundational bricks in your family's "wall." Talk about putting a positive spin on a family meeting! This is part of building the history that your stepfamily needs. This is building memories that will bring continuity for years to come.

How will you keep your marriage the priority in light of Those People? How will you keep your marriage in first position? Children can easily become the focus of the marriage and family, leaving the couple which

is to be the foundational anchor to the family appallingly neglected. It is this very spirit that gave birth to the byline, *"If you ain't got the marriage you ain't got nothin.'"*

Remarried couples will have their foundation and commitment to one another chipped away by those they love the most (Those People). Creating an atmosphere of trust and honesty has to be the bedrock of the family. During all phases of childhood and even young adulthood, if the kids have experienced a divorce, the two core issues of trust and honesty have been torn apart.

Stop and think about your previous family. There may have been a progression of peacefulness, then manipulation, next volatility, ending in the final stages of a great train wreck. Since you've taken the time to be restored as a person, a loving committed remarriage gives the kids an opportunity to observe and participate in a healthy family situation.

This can bring a new way of looking at marriage for children of all ages. Will they learn how to relate in a healthy manner to others, in

> *Life lessons are often better caught than taught.*

preparation for their own husband and wife relationships, by observing you in your new remarriage? If you have taken the steps to heal by experiencing God's grace, the platform is ready for Those People to have an entry to the process.

Life lessons are often better caught than taught. Therefore, the concepts that have been shared for you and your new spouse to utilize can be passed on to your kids at their level of understanding and application. Think about the terms shared and how you can use each of them

effectively with all your kids.

Consider how these terms relate to your kids:

Open Doors: Mental associations to their past

Bare Wires: Emotional connections to their earlier period

Sneaker Waves: Situational links to what went before

Old Tapes/New Tapes: Old actions and thoughts of what to expect as children

Short Accounts: Rebuilding trust as a tool of being honest with one another

Foxholes: Where they know and trust you aren't going anywhere!

SHARE THESE CONCEPTS WITH YOUR KIDS!

End of Chapter Questions

1. List two major differences between the two households your children travel between.

   _____

   _____

   _____

2. How have these differences affected your marriage?

   _____

   _____

   _____

3. How well do you know your child's heart? Start today by asking intentional questions to learn more; study and listen to their responses.

_____

_____

_____

4. What pink elephant issues are you living with right now? How about any unresolved ones from the past?

_____

_____

_____

5. Is your home warm, safe, and inviting for your stepkids? Ask them what they think.

_____

_____

_____

6. What traditions have collided in your household? Which ones have complemented each other? Look at the next holiday coming up. What new tradition can you create? Make it a family conversation!

_____

_____

_____

7. On a scale of 1-10 (1 being lowest), how is your plan for discipline going for you? How can you improve your situation?

    _____

    _____

    _____

8. Plan a "Triple F Night" (Forced Family Fun). Let your kids plan it! (Be ready for anything!)

    _____

    _____

    _____

9. Hold a family "meeting" and work on the TEAM acronym.

    _____

    _____

    _____

Action Item:

Time for a date for just the two of you! Do something romantic. Ladies, you plan it!

"Spoil your spouse...not your children."

—Unknown

RESTORED & Remarried

Chapter 8

Teens, Adult Children, and Grandparents

Chapter 8

Teens, Adult Children, and Grandparents

*Those Who Know,
Those Who Think They Know,
and Grandparents Who Really Do Know*

Teenagers

Did we mention that when we first got married we were crazy about each other? To this day we are still crazy in love and enjoy our marriage daily. The biggest challenges when we first got married revolved around Those People, who at the time were in the majority and teenagers at that! Two adult kids out of the house, three teens, and two pre-teens

were in and out of the home with duffle bags in tow, sticky shoes, muddy clothes, and an "a-teen-tude!"

Brenda and I were enjoying ourselves. Why weren't the kids? Yeah, they were traveling between two countries, but we thought our place was pretty cool. We tried our level best to make everyone comfortable while also keeping their schedules as close to normal as before the remarriage. Mix in teenage attitudes, emotions, and feeding frenzies, and we often felt like we were pushing a ton of rocks up a hill.

Some of our early attempts at bonding brought us laughs, even today. And we quickly learned that one of the best ways to bond a family is to go camping.

I (Brenda) had a tent trailer that we decided to take to the Oregon coast one summer. The kids (all teens at the time) were excited to get out in the woods. Conversations of who was the biggest pyromaniac ensued. And of course, there would be incredible sand dunes to jump from as they were working on their skateboarding skills.

We got to the campground and found our site. My kids jumped out to help Gil guide the tent trailer into our "home" for the weekend. Gil's kids ran off to check out where the bathrooms were and all there was to do. My kids were really concerned about backing this trailer in. "Does Gil know how to do this? Is he going to hit the tree? Watch out for the electrical outlet!" Although Gil had done this a million times and was good at it, my kids were freaking out. Gil's kids were oblivious to their concern. They had seen their dad do this a million times.

I appreciate how organized Gil is. He is Mr. Prepared. I must admit I value an organized campsite too. We got everything settled and had a wonderful dinner. As we were setting the boys up in tents, Gil asked for help putting up a tarp over the trailer and the tent. Gil's kids were ready to help. My kids said, "Why do we have to do this? It's not going to rain. This is a waste of time." Yet they were respectful and helped.

About one or two in the morning we heard it. Drip, drip, and then light filled the tents and the sky roared. Then, you got it, a huge downpour. As we all woke up and checked to make sure we were dry, all were OK and we went back to bed. In the morning my boys sheepishly said,

"Gee, that was a good idea putting up that tarp. We would have been soaked! Now we see why you did that, Gil. Thanks."

We still laugh today at the downpour that was not supposed to happen. That was one of the first steps of trust my guys had with Gil.

> *Why do we have to do this?*
> *It's not going to rain.*
> *This is a waste of time.*

We came up with the term "The Triple F Night" (Forced Family Fun) to create events to connect with each of our children. These were family activities designed to create bonding moments they may have had as biological children, but not with one another.

In a way, our kids were aware of one another before we were married. They had seen one another at church over the years. But it was quite another matter to live in the same house together. Awkward or just out of place would be words for the early stages of adjustments. At first, they all had the idea this would be fun.

We wanted them to bond to the new family and to us, but it was all contradictory to where they were developmentally. The Triple F Night and other outings we could do together were met with, "I don't wanna go!" or "Boring!" Thus, came the term "Forced Family Fun." We required all to participate. Usually our plans were accepted and everyone enjoyed the activity after the fact. Plus, they did gain relationships with one another.

The kids were trying to move away from the family and parents during these lovely teenage years. It is a natural part of growing up. As parents, we had to learn to relax and not force participation as a fine line of

their individuality. But at the same time we did not want to allow them to avoid connecting with their new siblings and stepparent. Reminding ourselves to remain calm and provide stability required us to keep in mind the crockpot mentality.

Don't force your kids to give up their social life. Instead, firmly encourage their involvement in the family life. History and relationships can't grow out of thin air. Taking on a project or conquering a problem together builds unity and respect for one another.

Taking time to learn about their culture and their friends is foundational as well. We have found that friends rule and influence our kids' choices. Don't get us wrong here. Teens do want their parents' approval. But friends are important as well. As best as possible, keep the home open to their friends. Do your best to be seen, but don't try to be one of the gang. As stepparents as well as parents of teens, engaging the kids or the mob of kids when they are at your house is best because then you know where they are.

Frankly, we think our kids are pretty great. Each one of them is unique and special in their own way. We also know that if we knew all the stuff our teen kids have done and never told us, we would freak out or lose more sleep just thinking about the "what ifs."

> # *R*elationships can't grow out of thin air.

To keep harmony in the stepfamily with kids traveling to and fro and the mixture of teen hormones, the only thing we found that kept the peace was an atmosphere of trust and honesty. Failures happen. Major lines of trust are crossed. Communication at times is horrible. Defaulting to trust and honesty with pink elephant meetings is our reliable safety net.

My (Brenda's) parents divorced when I was fifteen years old. Being an only child, I didn't have any siblings to share my feelings with. At that point I felt closer to my mom and spent more time with her. I remember feeling terrible for my dad, since my mom had left him. I felt powerless as he walked through the aftermath of his train wreck. Although my memory isn't very good, I do remember being awfully focused on myself. School was consuming; a new boyfriend and my goal to tour with the Ice Capades was on the forefront of my mind. Maybe I was hiding because I didn't want to deal with my parents' pain…and mine.

Two summers later, I was on the road with the Ice Capades. My dad remarried. I had met Jeannie only once before they were married in Las Vegas. She brought two girls into that marriage who were four and six years old at the time. I never really had a close relationship with them. I was eighteen years old and living independently. When I would go over to see them, I always felt like a visitor. Everyone was kind, but I never felt I could just go look in the refrigerator. I felt like my dad had started this new family and I was just an onlooker. I knew he loved me, but never could put into words how I felt. Maybe I was just scared.

Things got better once I had my own kids. My relationship with Jeannie improved tremendously. There was a new, fresh focus—my kids. It was like a brand-new point for our relationship. Neither of us had this experience before with these kids! I felt Jeannie showed her love to me through my kids, which was fine with me! Jeannie passed away several years ago, before Gil and I met. There are so many times now that I wish I could pick her brain. How did she really feel as a stepmom? What pitfalls should I look out for as a stepmom? Now that I am older, I feel like we could have had some really significant, authentic conversations. I'm finally old enough to process them now!

God had a sense of humor when He created teenagers. Do you suppose it was because He could laugh at their parents as they pull their hair out trying to connect with them—just like He is with us sometimes? Of course, this is a generalization. I know some of you have great relationships with your teenagers. (Don't let your friends know. They will be very jealous.) There are healthy parts of being a teen and many unhealthy parts. The same goes with parenting your teen.

One part that is most unsettling is the fact that teens are pulling away from us. They want to be independent. They want their own friends. They want to make their own decisions and make their own rules. This is normal and, when done correctly, will mold them into adults who will contribute positively to our communities. Now, when I say "done correctly," that doesn't mean that they always make correct decisions. Bad decisions with a terrible consequence can be just what the doctor ordered for that teen to learn a life lesson.

Do you realize that the average human brain does not finish developing until the age of twenty-five? So when we ask our teens, "What were you thinking? Have you lost your whole mind?" We're asking the wrong question. Technically, they have only a partially formed brain to lose!

Let's take a quick look at teen culture today:

Teen Stats:

- 750,000 girls get pregnant each year—34 percent before age twenty[1]

- 75 percent of teenagers' first sexual experience involves alcohol[2]

- Marijuana today is twice as potent as it was twenty years ago[3]

- Average age of exposure to pornography is between eight and eleven years old (while doing their homework on the Internet)[4]

- 70 percent of TV shows have some sexual content[5]

- Teens say they want to hear from their parents to save sex (and sexual activity) for marriage (more than from media and their peers)[6]

Our teens and tweeners are under incredible pressure, far beyond what we had to contend with when we were their age. They are battling every day with their self-image, and with pressure to have sex, do drugs, keep their grades up, and stay on the team. You throw in the whole stepfamily scenario and that can add dynamite to their already volatile

world. We may be the only voice in their lives that is supportive and encouraging. We need to have them feel that they play a significant part in our family. In the same breath, we need to give them their space. We want them to grow up and be independent adults who positively contribute to society.

> *What were you thinking? Have you lost your whole mind?*

We need to recognize and validate a teen's need for independence. It is your job to be that safe place for them to test their boundaries and spread their wings. It's OK if they trip up once in awhile. Short of death, I think consequences are better than all the talking, shouting, and "discussions" we can ever have. Let them understand and experience the importance of family. And, as a stepparent, realize that you may not be best buddies right now. And that is reasonable. Remember: let them set the pace. You're not going anywhere, right? I guarantee that patience will win out.

In the midst of the adventure of raising teenagers, please do not forget:

> *If you ain't got the marriage, you ain't got nothin'.*

There is one key we cannot forget while we're "slow cooking" our stepfamily and exercising intentional parenting. In general, most kids did not ask you to divorce or remarry. Your marriage represents another loss to them: the loss of their previous family. See their new family through their eyes and it will hopefully bring you to a new level of compassion for their feelings. When harsh attitudes appear, we have learned to ask this question (before being thrown into a tizzy) first:

*Is this a teenage thing, a girl thing, a hormone thing, a
divorce thing, or a remarriage thing?*

Are their reactions or attitudes reflective of one of the places they are
in life? Even in intact families, teens undergo hormonal changes and
"warm and fuzzy" is nowhere in sight! Try to survey the terrain with
your teen before you assume this is all about you and the stepfamily!

Adult Children

Children grow up, or at least they get older! When couples remarry, the
children in their lives may be young adults and on their own. They are
members of the family with whom stepparents may never connect. If
they do connect, it could be on a very limited basis. On the other hand,
defenses may be so high that the grown child chooses to disconnect,
avoid, and politely disengage all together. They may decide to cut
themselves off from a relationship that you desire as a parent.

An older child may feel completely cut off if the newly remarried
couple has their own children. As a stepsibling, they are not included
into welcoming the new addition. There are books shedding more light
on this topic and can be referenced at your local library or on the
Internet. Check out the Resource list at the back of this book. The
vital point to be aware of here is that this too can affect your marriage
and can create sadness, anger, and conflict.

Circumstances may have it that the newly remarried couple could be
getting in each other's way. They may be hindering the other's ability
to have a healthy relationship with their own kids. You may recall
that divorce does not end family dynamics. It just places them in two
different households.

Now to stepparents of adult stepkids—relax! You cannot force
a stepchild who is in his/her twenties or thirties to mow the lawn
any more than you can force a stranger. Frankly, you would not even
consider asking a stranger to mow your lawn if he was an adult. That
is our point here. These (adult) people are adults. Adult children have
passed the point where you can give orders as a parental figure. You are
now a step-parental figure who has no relationship or built-in respect

and love to bank upon. Add the dynamics of the husband, wife, or partner your adult child brings into the family, and we're talking about some complex issues.

You also can't disregard the older child's ability to sort out or add to the dynamics (negatively or positively). This alone can put the relationship at an extremely different and complex level. Showing respect and love for them as adults will hopefully build bridges for them to love you back. I am so glad that Brenda and I encourage each other to nurture separately and together as a couple the relationships with each one of Those People.

> *Children grow up, or at least they get older.*

Remember, according to studies, males handle divorce better than females and females handle remarriage worse than males. This is even more vividly apparent in the fact that children at this age have the legal right to choose. They can choose a relationship with their mother or their father, or neither.

Here is what one of our kids shared (age nineteen when we got married, twenty-six now):

> *"I believe how the remarriage affects older children depends on how close they live to their parents and how close they were to the individual bio parent in the first place. As for myself, I was the middle child and the peace keeper. I always felt mutual love, acceptance, and bonding with both bio parents. This is why in high school and the first year in college I would switch back and forth from one parent's side of opinion to the other's; trying to figure out for myself*

which one was really in the wrong or trying to pick apart which one was lying or hiding something. Believe me, it was a very large mind game! I thought I had developed a unique system of picking apart why they got divorced, but realized later on in my early twenties that it was really just a huge game of who was the better parent, which is impossible to decide, let alone as an adult! It takes a long time, and even impossible to some, to realize that no parent is better than the other. The only thing that really will decipher which parent is better is who shows true love for the child. I was lucky to have both parents who truly showed love for me and my siblings.

Overall, the remarriage was a little hurtful at the time since I was young and the divorce was still fresh in my mind. Nevertheless, now that I look back as an adult and a little wiser, I see Brenda's kids in the wedding picture to support their mom, but with the absence of me and my siblings there to support my father. I feel sad and remorseful for being absent in such a huge step for my father. But the family pictures since then have somewhat made up for it."

Sons and daughters may gravitate toward the mom or the dad for whatever reasons. A lack of relationship can be the polite excuse, but you know as well as we do that battle lines exist within the shreds of the old family structure. Bio parents may still attempt to create loyalties that grown children usually can see through. It can cause resentment. If one of the parents is taking this approach, it is no longer just "rocks in their buckets." Instead, it is rocks in the head of the parent for such foolishness.

Grown children can be haunted by unfinished business that was divisive to their family of origin.

Hurts that wound the heart of the child are still embedded long into adulthood. We may have forgotten harsh words or lashing out at the kids during the fallout of the divorce, but they don't forget. Trust me.

According to statistics I (Gil) have regarding fathers, it seems that age tends to separate dads from their kids as time goes forward. Not that

I'm picking on us dads entirely, but truth be told, we dads tend to go to our cave and stuff away the pain we know our kids have endured. It's easier to hide from the pain that you didn't or couldn't fix, rather than try to address it.

Whether we inflicted that pain or the mother was more to blame, no one cares at this point. Reach out! Start by asking for their forgiveness. Lead them through the path of reconciliation. And all along, be prepared, they still may choose not to accept and rudely snuff your efforts.

I desire to stay connected to my own children and their present and future children, as well as building a relationship with my stepchildren. I know this is a long-time endeavor. It is a fine line of "pestering" and "staying in touch." Seeing a biological child only once a year is a crime, and it's the most unloving message you could possibly send to your kids. Your lack of contact, much less lack of effort, is frankly unloving. They may be wrapped up in their own careers, families, and pursuits. You may be further down their list of priorities. But believe me, they will always remember your efforts. When they are your age they will keep in mind the fact that you at least tried to keep in touch. That goes a long way.

You may offer time and love and not be taken up on the offer. If this happens, step back and accept what is offered in return. Build upon whatever portion of time they are willing to give. As time goes by and as we grow older, the channels of communication will have a chance to serve all. In the lyrics of a song, "Say What You Need to Say," John Mayer nails the matter on the head. Getting issues out on the table is far too important. None of us know when our time is up.

Here is what one of our kids shared (age nineteen when we got married, twenty-six now):

> *"I never felt pressured into forming a relationship with you (Brenda). The only stress on the relationship was getting to know another motherly figure that was so different to what I was accustomed too. I will be very utmost with you and honest. I will never take you for my mother in place of my own (which I know you already know), but I will accept*

*you as a different kind of parent—one that is not quite as personal, but definitely in the know! You have known me long enough to see my quirks, dreams, and downfalls. You are indisputably part of my life and I love that. If stepfamilies are to work, it will only work with people that are willing to accept the whole baggage! **And you have! Thank you.***

I appreciate both of you guys for being open to my agnostic faith and judgments. Overall I believe in love, a faith in a higher power, and unbiased listening. You both display this with your walks in a higher spiritual power. This makes you both whole and receiving."

When I (Gil) have heard of fathers who only see their kids two or three times a year out of choice, I stop and wonder what is with that attitude. Sure, if the child is an adult and lives far away because of career or their own choices, that may make sense. But to not drop a call to keep a line open because of the stepfamily factor is shortsighted. Today's technology may not be face-to-face contact, but it is contact and may be a place to start and keep using. You never know, your adult children's children may want, need, and cherish a relationship with a set of loving grandparents. Will you be there to offer it?

> *Start by asking for their forgiveness.*

I (Gil) find it really cool when my kids contact Brenda before me. I love it when I get a contact from one of my stepsons as well. Weekly phone calls are a method I learned from a mentor of mine, Jack MacKay. Sunday nights he'd give a call to all the kids just to say hi or leave a message. Sometimes it would be every other week, but the call was made to keep the channels open.

We have learned to adjust expectations. We know that our relationship with adult kids will be different because of age, distance, and the natural affinity for them becoming adults and living their own lives. We look for the "wins," so to say, when a positive connection occurs. Those moments build history and a foundation for the future. When looking for relational steps to be reciprocated, we have seen more with some kids, less with others. You just can't get hung up on that.

It is pure joy when you come to accept your children where they are in their lives and situations. This also allows us to relax and diffuse tensions. We take time to participate in their interests and gifting as much as possible, while we also develop our own lives. A healthy "us" that shows interest in each of them, we believe, will make way for growth that will impact the here and now in addition to the future.

Gil's oldest son was twenty-two years old when we got married. He was already on his own. There was very little interaction between him and me (Brenda). When we did have time together it was in a group situation and he was always polite. I wanted so much to have a closer relationship with him. I could see the unsettledness in his spirit and I honestly just hurt for him. I wanted to have a heart-to-heart with him and love on him. That was my desire. Communicating was a different story.

I would try so hard not to say the wrong thing and never had the time in person to convey my feelings. As much as I don't like communicating via email (I like the eye contact), this was an avenue with him I was willing to try. Most kids that age communicate via email anyway! Why not with their stepmom?

I remember the first time I emailed Josh. It was short and sweet. As I hit the send button I felt my heart racing. Would he blow me off? Would he welcome my note? Was I bugging him?

When I received his note back, I was able to breathe a sigh of relief. It was very short and sweet as well. Nothing deep, but I wasn't looking for that. Just the fact that he recognized my existence was a win for me. *I may be making much more out of this than he is, I thought, but I want him to know that I care.*

This is an ongoing process and that's OK. Why? You should know the mantra by now! Because **I'm not going anywhere**. I'm in this for the long haul. My desire is to love on my stepkids whether they return that love or not. It's the right thing to do and it's what Christ has called us to do!

> # This was going to be very bittersweet.

Off to the Races

We love the racetrack analogy. Here's how it goes. Picture yourself in a stadium. Around the football field is a track. You see your child (any age, teen to adult) running around the track. This represents them living their life. You are cheering from the stands. Some kids will stop and catch their breath with you (conversation) and grab a drink (encouragement). Then they are off again.

Some kids just keep on running. You see them stop and talk to others, but not you. Oh, they know you're there, but they run on by. This can be painful as the cheerleader. Even when everyone else has left the stadium, you are called to continue to stand. On those sometimes rare moments, when that kid comes by to catch their breath, or when he/she needs a drink, you'll be there. And that's what counts.

Here is what one of our kids shared (age nineteen when we got married, twenty-six now):

> *"The most secure part of your guys' testimony is to love on the kids no matter what. Stick with that and run with it. It literally saved my life."*

Down the Aisle

When your children get married, you enter yet another season. Now, some of you may have already stepped into this stage of life, and for others it may be many years away. My (Brenda's) oldest son got married last summer. I knew this was going to be new territory for all of us, in a lot of ways.

The details of the wedding came together quite nicely. I can say that with confidence because being the mother of the groom I didn't have to do a lot! My soon-to-be daughter-in-law knew that this was more about the marriage than the wedding. Bravo, Laurie! No bridezilla here.

Months ahead, I knew I needed to prepare myself emotionally. This was going to be very bittersweet. I was thrilled that my son was getting married. Yet, I had always dreamed of my ex and I sitting in the front row…together. I had never thought we'd be sitting at different ends of the row with various people between us. Then complicated thoughts of who would be in what pictures went through my mind. There weren't a lot of clean lines of relationships. It was hard on my son too, trying to accommodate everyone.

From the very beginning of the preparation for the wedding, and the wedding itself, I kept a phrase in the forefront of my mind: "It's all about the kids." Because I stood on that hill from the very beginning, I'm hoping I made it easier for my son. It was a lovely day. Everyone made it through without any big faux pas. But here are a few thoughts I know I will keep in mind for the next wedding:

1. As much as you can prepare emotionally, be ready for some Sneaker Waves. There may be some tsunamis too. My Sneaker Wave was seeing all these different people from various times in my life. There were good memories, and it was cool that they came to support my son. But what a barrage of emotion seeing people from "my old life" and people from "my new life" in the same room!

2. If there are still some Bare Wires from the ex that are found easily, watch where everyone is seated at the reception. Stay on your best behavior, no matter what!

3. Are there new spouses, girlfriends/boyfriends, or partners involved? Be cordial and nice, no matter what!

4. What to wear? Ladies, you might be put at ease if the moms (step/bio/future in-law) know what each other is wearing ahead of time. As the stepmom, I would tend to stay in the background unless otherwise asked.

Bottom line: It's not about you! It's about your child. Your child's wedding should be one of the happiest days of their life. Remember, you are the adult. You may have to "suck it up" for a little while, but aren't your kids worth it?

My (Gil's) oldest son got married two months after Brenda and me. Although Brenda wasn't invited to the wedding, we both agreed I needed to be there. As the father of the groom and later as the stepfather of the groom (at my new son's wedding), I took a posture of serving my "son" any way I could. They were excited and stressed at the same time. I felt like a guest and a member of the family at the same time. I chose to keep things light-hearted. I encouraged them privately. I shared special memories with them. And I made sure there was a lot of laughter.

Reflecting on those days, concerned about their own family's future success or failure, having a father/stepfather who remains steadfast goes a long way. Anticipate a moment where a reassuring word will need to be shared to help calm the affects of innuendos of their family's great train wreck.

Grandparents

In a secret agent movie, I (Gil) once heard a relationship matrix that goes like this:

A friend of your friend could be your enemy.

An enemy of your friend could be your enemy.

A friend of your enemy could be your friend.

But an enemy of an enemy could be a friend.

> *Espionage wouldn't
> be the best description.*

Espionage would not best be the description of how we relate to our parents or former in-laws, but the rendition in how they relate to us and our former spouse can be just as convoluted.

How was your relationship with your parents and your ex when you were married? How is it now? What is your relationship like with your ex-in-laws after the great train wreck? At best, it might be a tight rope of treason between them and you and your ex. This all sounds messy, and in reality it is!

It is said that blood is thicker than water and, as a result, parents will most of the time side with their own flesh and blood. But then again, that is not always the case. A parent can support the son or daughter-in-law when their flesh and blood is really messing up. Add grandchildren to the mix, and the grandparents may stay loyal to their child or the spouse or both whether right or wrong, for the sake of the grandkids.

The benefits of family, once enjoyed by an in-law relationship, cuts both ways. Once trusting, open relatives shut down overnight, sometimes never to be opened again. Where our culture sees more grandparents involved with the raising of grandchildren, is it any wonder that anyone can get through the complicated lines of communication to authentic connections? Principles of forgiveness and accepting the former in-law on level terms is a balancing act, but if possible, it is best for the

kids of your former marriage.

A comparison/contrast in our situation finds a lot of the above complex associations to be true. To be honoring of our in-laws and ex-in-laws, I will leave the following to suffice as illustration by asking you a couple of questions:

How would you feel about accepting an invitation from your current wife's former in-laws for a weekend stay?

If an attempt to reach out to your former in-laws to reconnect on a friendly level is rejected, how would you feel, especially when you had been close for years?

The primary reason for addressing this issue on grandparents is that many of them want to be recognized in the overall scheme of the family structure. Different cultural backgrounds have their own strengths and weaknesses in their family structure. How/where the grandparents fit in can very much be tied to that. But culture aside, divorce is still just as heartbreaking for the grandparents, especially if their relationship with their grandchildren is negatively impacted.

Honoring our elders may not even be a thought as we are too wrapped up in our own "thing." But recalling the pain my (Gil's) own dad shared with me, watching me go through the divorce process, gave me a clue that I was not the only one in pain.

What a joy it was to share with him the healing process I had to go through. And then, what an even greater joy to introduce Brenda, first as a friend, then as my fiancé, and eventually as my new wife.

"Stretching" is the best way I (Gil) can describe meeting Brenda's former in-laws. I was pleasantly surprised at how quickly they accepted me. As I grow older, less surprises me when God's grace is shared in loving extensions of family. The family tree in the stepfamily scenario is more like a forest. And these strange but true tales, I'm sure, would pale in comparison to your stories. Please share with us, if you wish, the joys and the sorrows of your experiences.

Listen to these thoughts from a stepmom/stepgrandma with over forty years of experience:

> *"Divorce and remarriage create new dynamics for so many families, but often the intergenerational and extended family ties are overlooked. Your kids and their grandparents, not to mention favorite aunts, uncles, and cousins, may have special relationships that tug at the young and much older hearts, more than you might ever imagine."*

> *"Grandchildren are the crown of old men, and the glory of sons is their fathers."*—**Proverbs 17:6**

How are you and your new blended family honoring the extended family ties? Are you giving sparkle to the crown of your parents, and your children's and stepchildren's grandparents?

Take a little time to read Proverbs and absorb some of the wisdom of King Solomon and his cronies. They offer some practical advice about the art of living in honesty and justice, and spell out some pitfalls to avoid along the way. You never know, maybe somewhere along the way one of your "aged people" or your child's extended family will be planting seeds to blossom in your new family.

End of Chapter Questions

1. Have you had a "Triple F Night" lately? Plan one, with the help of the kids.

   _____

   _____

   _____

2. Do you have teens in the house (or nearby)? Don't be afraid to engage them in conversation about "their world." Ask them, sincerely, what is it like to be a teen now? What happens in the hallways at school? How common is sexual activity?

   _____

   _____

   _____

3. As the bio parent, if you have adult children, how can you nurture the relationship between them and your spouse?

_____

_____

_____

4. As the stepparent of adult children, how are you supporting your spouse's relationship with their kids? How are you reaching out to them yourself? Can you improve? Ask your spouse.

_____

_____

_____

5. Are there any grandchildren involved? Is there a healthy balance in favoritism between all the grandkids? Total spoilation, for all, right?

_____

_____

_____

6. On a scale of 1-10 (1 being low, 10 being high) where would you put your relationship with your ex-in-laws? For the sake of the kids, does it need to improve?

_____

_____

_____

7. Have you acknowledged the hurt your ex-in-laws might feel from their child's (your ex's) divorce?

_____

_____

_____

Action Item:

Treat yourself to a peanut buster parfait (or an ice cream of your choice). You deserve it!

"If love is blind, why is lingerie so popular?"

—Unknown

Chapter 9

Sex and Money

Chapter 9

Sex and Money

More Than Splitting the Sheets and a Checkbook

Sex

How many of you skipped to this chapter first? Yeah, me (Gil) too! As men, sex and money are two of the hottest topics. They have the potential to bring a lot of pleasure or they can create havoc. For men, sex tends to be top priority. It's just the way we are wired. Of course, a women's desire for sex can be just as high a priority, but for an entirely different set of reasons. Mix in the issues that remarriage poses with both sex and money and now you have the makings of some interesting issues.

Candidly, I (Gil) didn't realize how hard it was going to be to write this chapter. I sat for a moment (two weeks) to get the process started with at least an opening statement, and I confess, I had to get my heart clear before putting my hands to the keyboard.

> ## Sex in marriage is an incredible gift.

To begin with, I'm a pretty conservative guy and, quite frankly, the issue of my sex life is none of anyone's business. The thought of sharing my heart, struggles, and joys of this side of my mind and relationship created a face-off with Old Tapes tied to Phantoms combined with Sneakers Waves washing over Bare Wires. I'll unpack those details as I write this chapter. But then Brenda had to remind me that I wasn't in this alone. Bring it on!

Sex in marriage is an incredible gift. As powerful as it is, it can also be easily derailed. We may have the best of intentions, then life ramps up.

The Bedroom

In her book *Surprised by Remarriage,*[1] Ginger Kolbaba writes about eight points that every remarried couple ought to be aware of when it comes to their new sex life. The following points are made by Ginger, but I (Gil) expanded on them:

1. **Kids kill spontaneity**—You could have sex anywhere and anytime at home if not for Those People. Sexual intimacy has little room when your home has a rotating front door with kids going in and out. It's OK to put a lock on your bedroom door!

2. **Guard your sex life**—Seize the moments of opportunity! Be creative!

3. **Guard your sex thought life**—Check all Old Tapes at the door. The sexual dimension of your new marriage is to be secure from any previous relationship. Don't allow any lingering thoughts to rob you now! Pornography is a marriage killer (more on that later).

4. **Talk about sex**—Sex is a form of communication. Did you realize that? Be honest about your likes and dislikes, what are your erogenous zones. If it's easier to write a note or letter or draw a picture for your spouse concerning sex, then do it! Believe it or not, guys are more sensitive about this issue than women. Guys need to know that their woman is satisfied. Ladies, do you let him know that? If you don't feel that way, help him along! Guys need to know if they have "conquered the hill" so to speak. The more you talk or communicate about sex, the more comfortable it becomes.

5. **Make foreplay an all-day event**—(Gil) On this issue, guys, learn her love language and become fluent with what communicates the fact that she is loved and cherished. It's not all about the sex; her strongest sex organ is her mind. Foreplay is getting her excited mentally for the "play." Your part is to be "nice to the girl," genuinely from the heart. There are so many different ways to communicate throughout

Sex is a form of communication.

the day: texting, email, and the old-fashioned ways of talking on the phone or leaving notes for each other. (Brenda) Ladies, are you being his "girlfriend" throughout the day? Would you want to come home to you?

6. **Schedule sex**—Interruptions such as jobs, kids, music lessons, sporting events, and paying the bills are just a few realities that are barriers to a regular sex life. Plan for sex and then enjoy! If you've prepared in advance, the plans actually can work into the "foreplay" category, allowing fun and satisfaction to increase.

7. **Know when to seek counseling**—Sex is a huge act of trust! If an ex had an affair, the ability to trust could be affecting your remarriage bedroom. A deep and intense pain is usually something that people need help working through. Sexual issues are no different; therefore, seek biblically sound counseling and accountability to achieve healing. Some backtracking is not to be taken personally but a matter of empathy that can make room for healing and health for the long haul.

Would you want to come home to you?

8. **Don't give up!**—If there are struggles or seeming impasses to your sex life, don't bury them. Pray about them for and with one another. Who created this whole sex stuff anyway? Christ wants our relationship in the bedroom to be wonderful. It is a special gift He has given us for each other. Adjust your expectations and let your prayer life take over your worries. Then allow the sparks to rekindle in one another's eyes. Then practice, practice, practice!

To summarize what Ginger Kolbaba makes clear to men and women alike—pray, even about your sex life. God is interested in that dimension of your new marriage too. He created it, you know!

Ladies, it's OK to initiate romance! Take a risk and buy something new to surprise your man. I haven't personally found any negligees in flannel, but who cares! They don't stay on very long anyway!

> # *Sex is a huge act of trust!*

What's his favorite color? Don't let your "less than perfect body" stop you from showing off what you have. Ladies (from Gil), it's not so much that you are a size "perfect," but that you willingly allow your sensuality to be expressed. Another tip I (Brenda) learned—keep your underwear "in good repair." Match your bra and panties too! Of course, this is personal preference! It's the little things that can keep a relationship fresh. Talk about it!

And guys, tell your woman she is beautiful. Sometimes women forget we are beautiful after a day when we've had spit-up on us, driven 100 miles in a car pool, or have worked 12 hours.

Your bedroom is a good thermometer as to how the rest of your relationship is going. If there are issues you are not addressing outside of your bedroom, the buck will stop there. That is why we encourage you to keep your relationship running "lean and mean." Keep short accounts! Don't be a poser. Don't hide behind the demands of the kids, work, or life. Keep your emotional channels of communication clear. If you don't, it will all come back to bite you in the bedroom. No one wins in the end.

Have you been exposed to a healthy discussion about sex while laughing at yourself? *Laugh Your Way to a Better Marriage*[2] is a fun way to enrich, as well as strengthen, your marriage. Issues other than sex are also addressed in this presentation that is available in person with Mark Gungor, with live and video presentations or DVDs that you can watch at home together.

The "keys to incredible sex" segment of the presentation unfolds right and wrong approaches to sex that men and women can relate to. Mark takes a quick census of how women see exclusiveness, its effect on how they view sex, and how the issue of pornography intrudes in the bedroom.

Pornography

Another way to address this topic is "what sex is or is not." First, *sex is not cyber sex* or viewing pornography. (Come on, guys, this statement should go without saying.) It continues to amaze me (Gil) how many marriages are breaking up as men and women are imposters to their spouse. I guess if things aren't going well in your relationship, having a virtual partner works; they don't talk back or disagree with you. But what happens when the person who is viewing porn finds this isn't as fulfilling anymore? They can move on to the real thing, have affairs, and/or develop other unhealthy associations or habits.

> *It is packaged to be very alluring.*

Revenues from the pornography industry are in the billions. Porn executives would not like you to know this, but research validates that porn can be an addictive behavior. Something that starts out as a curious exploration on the Internet can launch you into some very unhealthy habits. Fueling this addictive behavior is directly related to the porn industry's bottom line through purchasing videos, buying from advertisers, sex toys, and more.

Do you realize that pornography photographers take between 6,000 and 22,000 pictures for a centerfold layout? The pictures that are chosen are then air brushed and photo-shopped. I (Brenda) have heard models say that they don't even look like their pictures because they have been touched up so much. The pictures of women we see in

magazines, on television, and in movies aren't always real. When it comes to porn, it's an illusion that is being sold. And not every man has a six pack…those can be airbrushed too!

> *Your body does not belong to you anymore; it belongs to your wife.*

Sexual addiction or being a prisoner to your sexual self-gratification is not a self-expression of love. You promised to keep yourself pure and give yourself to no other. Do you recall that "commitment" in your vows? And, ladies, you are not off the hook either. The number of women lost in the fantasy of porn is on the rise. Romantic novels and daytime television have helped propel women into this hole. Take television, for example. A simple kiss or a hug seen on television years ago would have made us blush. The sexual innuendos and outright soft porn seen today on prime time is accepted as normal and expected. We even have ratings for the levels of "normalcy."

Pornographers have actually added more emotion to their story lines to attract women. Women are more sensitive to the emotion and relationships in the stories and men are caught up in the images they see. It is packaged to be very alluring. Society, whether you are in or out of the church, has bought the lie that porn is OK. It doesn't hurt anyone. Think again.

If you are a Bible-believing Christian, let me refresh your memory of your sexual commitment from 1 Corinthians 7. The text clearly states that your body does not belong to you anymore; it belongs to your wife and she needs sexual fulfillment just as much as you!

Recently I (Gil) spoke to a young woman who was a client of mine as well as a dear friend's daughter. She came in to make changes to

her auto insurance and wanted to see me personally. (It was upon her parent's recommendation.) I thought this rather strange for a minor change until I found it was to delete her husband from the policy. She had just finalized a divorce.

This was a young couple whom I knew fairly well and actually attended their wedding a few short years ago. They had two small children under the age of five, good jobs, and from all appearances seemed quite happy. Behind the scenes this young man/father and husband had issues with pornography that strangled his marriage and killed their sex life. Eventually, an impasse came where he chose his attraction to the other "fake cyber women and masturbation" to his real wife and mother of his children.

Me, Myself, and I

Next, *sex is not masturbation!* Since when is your hand more sensual than your woman's body? Your wife's body was designed for your exclusive pleasure. But, you may say, "I can't get the same stimulation!" To that I reply, "That is a major problem that was created by you; so what are you going to do about it?"

Yes, I agree it is a real issue! A woman's body may not be able to achieve the intense pressure you desire, but if your body has been conditioned to one method of sexual arousal and release, then it can be re-conditioned. Gentlemen, there are dozens of biblically sound resources for you to get this issue "straightened out" in your head and heart. Honestly, does masturbation really satisfy you emotionally and physically?

My point here is that men generally, and women to some extent, can be pulled into a prison of false security that does not require them to be emotionally engaged with one another. Two of the highest forms of selfishness are to ignore this issue of sex or use it as a weapon to get your way. Both motivations are unhealthy and if either were in your experience from the past, then Bare Wires are tangling everywhere!

Please, I implore you, don't enter a remarriage with these essential wires ignored. If you are into a remarriage, then seek help as soon

as possible. Do it for your own sake, let alone for all your extended family. There are reputable and confidential counseling services in most communities.

Putting the past in the past truthfully is easier said than done. Our recommendation is to get clear of misconceptions immediately. Building trust in the bedroom is foundational. Hazards of comparisons are traps and choosing not to fall into them may need intentional effort. Focus on the fact that "it's about us now!"

Phantoms, even of the slightest inclination, are enough to derail a great sex life. As scary as it may be to encounter a Phantom in this area of your relationship, ask questions that you feel you need to know to build trust between the two of you now. Then move forward and don't look back. You are now using DVDs and Blu-rays, not Old Tapes.

Phantoms will appear behind Open Doors that you least expect. As you risk opening the doors to your heart, I guarantee Sneaker Waves will follow. Your wall will be slammed against and it will feel like an explosion that you'd rather avoid.

> *I implore you, don't enter a remarriage with these essential wires ignored.*

Realize that deep healing in the area of sexuality will call upon you to offer forgiveness to yourself or your spouse, or whoever caused you harm. Do not withdraw. Sexual issues are connected to the core of a person. Rifts in the soul and personality, when encountering these deep issues, can extract anger, fear, discomfort, insecurity, and one's most important ability to trust.

It may be difficult to face off with Phantoms, Open Doors, or Sneaker Waves and how these all connect to Bare Wires. But I (Gil) acknowledge that after gaining perspective and healing in these sensitive areas, the sexual experience got even better.

Another thought here, because it fits with how I felt about opening up on this topic—it was like I was opening a box of TNT (dynamite) in a dark room with a lit match.

To me, it was a choice better left in the box than taking the risk to explore (trust) my heart to Brenda. Would I find new freedom by getting close enough to the TNT to know if it would explode? I found that TNT (Trusting Naked Truth) in the here and now could explode, but the risk outweighed the chances taken to connect even deeper emotionally in the present marriage. This new marriage is just that— new! It is what you make it out to be. And if you allow the past to leak into the present, you lose twice.

> *Bonding sexually is a life-long process between a husband and wife.*

Past choices and experiences will interface with the deepest desire a couple shares—that of an exclusiveness that was dashed against the rocks of divorce. Now, in remarriage "trust and honesty" are being rebuilt. This is not the time to get stuck in what was, but enjoy what is! Bonding sexually is a life-long process between a husband and wife. We are both made differently, physically and emotionally. It will take a lifetime to figure each other out, if that is even possible. This should keep things exciting and always new! Rebuilding this important area of your life takes time and if the attitude is one of, "I'm not going anywhere," then relax and enjoy the journey.

Getting away to make time for the fun factor or shared recreation is as important as making time for "making out." The affects of friendship in marriage truly show respect and admiration for each other. At risk of repeating myself (Gil), do you know one another's Love Language (Quality Time, Acts of Service, Physical Touch, Gifts, and Words of Affirmation)? Can you name the top two without a second thought or having to ask your spouse? If not, you have some homework.

Friends know each other's love languages. And lovers are better lovers because *sex is* an extension of loving the person at all possible levels.

Let me put it this way—the more aspects you learn about each other or explore together, the deeper connection you will share with your spouse. As a result, the better the sex. Yes, prayer (i.e., the spiritual facet) is the deepest connection possible because it is here that a person will be the most vulnerable.

When a husband and wife pray together, they both become vulnerable. We will know each other at a level no one else can share. We've found that the effects of a spiritual connection and prayer often result in a better sex life.

Money

Remarriage is fun and serious business at the same time. Each of us brings assets and financial obligations to a remarriage. If you are contemplating remarriage, have a good business mind. Run a credit check as well as a blood test before you remarry. Issues of money and health are two factors that require absolute trust. If you get any negative vibe or feedback on either of these two factors, apply the brakes. No emotional, feel-good fuzziness can substitute for the consequences of a bad decision in these life issues. Get perception checks, outside advice, or seek counsel if you've the slightest feeling of wrongness here.

One of the first couples we interviewed on this issue was having a "cold war" of sorts over a possession brought into the new marriage/stepfamily. At the time, a big screen television was all the rage and this new stepdad had a possessiveness that was unhealthy and harmful

around his toy. Granted, it was a luxury he enjoyed and it should be respected. But the attitude that crept into the family and ultimately the marriage caused an incredibly large issue, possession vs. people. (You will always lose when you put possessions over people.) The effects of this struggle penetrated how money got spent on his kids and her kids, even down to the choice of his checkbook and her checkbook.

Possession vs. people...

It's a fact that people bring with them habits of handling money and possessions through different experiences. Family of origin issues and characteristics can be explored by surveys such as a Couple Check-up and Prepare & Enrich, as we discussed in Chapter 1. You can also discuss the following questions:

1. While growing up, who brought home a paycheck, Mom or Dad or both?

2. Who paid the bills, Mom or Dad or both?

3. In your previous marriage, were there two paychecks coming in?

4. Who was more comfortable handling the money?

5. Are you a spender or a saver?

6. If you were single, how did you feel about money issues?

7. How did it go when you were preparing a budget?

8. Was a budget even involved?

Maybe the money was so tight due to paying child support, or the lack

of child support, that you learned to live on next to nothing. It doesn't really matter where you are with this whole topic of money. The most important thing is that you are flat-out honest! What did you like about how you did money stuff before or what were some habits or issues that created problems? Discuss both perspectives to find useful best practices (talk about a risk manager insurance agent term!) from the past for the here and now.

I (Brenda) feel much more comfortable working with money that Gil does. That is not a slam on Gil, but my life experience and past careers have allowed me to work in different financial environments. When we sit down together to pay bills, I can just see the anxiety in Gil's countenance. Frankly, I would find it frustrating as well. He is the man of the house. He is supposed to know how to handle all this, which is tied to me feeling protected and taken care of and cherished. He is my knight in shining armor who will battle all these pieces of paper before us and ride us off into the sunset filled with romance. OK, a little over the top, but ladies, do you agree with me? It may be unrealistic, but most of us can associate with this deep-down thought process.

Guys, maybe this makes a little more sense why your woman may get upset with you when you can't talk about money issues and come to some agreements. There are strings of security and safety connected to this issue, especially if your wife had the experience of being a single mom or was in a marriage where money was not dealt with on a foundation of trust and honesty.

Bare Wires and Old Tapes are very common in this area of a remarriage relationship. Share those with each other. It's about us now. Remember that money is a very important topic. It's one of the top five reasons for divorce. So get this cleared up early on.

Because trust has been proven and tested in this area of our relationship, when Gil and I sit down to pay bills it's not as stressful. We have learned to take the strengths and weaknesses each other has to offer and we come out pretty balanced. Of course a glass of wine doesn't hurt either!

For those of you who have all the kinks worked out in this area, you are in the minority. But good job! Keep these money points in mind to share with others. If money is a "growth area," that can be a "red flag." Get it resolved before you say "I do" that second or third time around. Love is not fiscally blind and stupid.

I (Gil) recall actually coming over to Brenda's to pay bills together before we got married. Now we were in the throes of remodeling her house, creating a space to call our own. We sat down the first time and discussed how we paid bills on a monthly system. Differences were very clear. I wrote checks for everything at the first of the month and she had several automatic withdrawals in place for regular bills. She had a debit card and I believed those type of financial tools were from hell. I was/am a "cold hard cash" type of guy. Talking through our differences and our "comfort zones" in this area, we both came to a point of agreement. Bottom line, we both had to be on the same page with our spending habits and savings plan.

We discussed how the checkbook would be handled. We even took the time and expense to sit down with a financial planner to uncover good and bad habits when managing our money. We met with people we trusted to help us design a budget. Then we met with others to critique the budget we had designed. We expressed our financial expectations openly, hoping to avoid arguments as best as possible.

> *A glass of wine doesn't hurt either!*

Money is still a hot topic now and then, but based on early agreements we mutually made, the issue or argument often has an emotional connection to the past...Old Tapes or Open Doors for example.

Juggling money in a remarriage will keep you on your toes. Make sure you take the time to look after your financial future too. We had to basically start from square one when we got remarried. We have

had to be very intentional about putting money aside for our future retirement. That has been hard, especially when dealing with kids. But it is possible.

> *Love is not fiscally blind and stupid.*

We observed how I (Gil) stressed about money while building the house extension. I must say Brenda was a brave and trusting woman to allow her home to be torn up and begin remodeling before the wedding had taken place. I still lived at my own place, and even though I signed onto the loan to make the expansion happen, I could have "bolted" and left her holding the bag. In the context of this book I must say to Brenda, thank you, once again, for trusting me!

The best way to handle the new situation is to start fresh. That way, there isn't territorialism as mentioned earlier. Everyone starts with a clean slate. In some situations, like ours, that was not financially possible. We recognized that with the kids, and did our best to make due with where God had us. Adding on to the house has given it a different feel, which has helped. Yet, Gil and I are looking forward to purchasing our own place someday. Remember in Chapter 2 when we stated that in remarriage the honeymoon comes at the end, when the kids are all out? It's never too late to go back and experience some of those important "firsts" at any point in your remarriage; they are not only fun but also foundational.

Kids and the Moolah

Early on, a major pitfall for our family was economic favoritism when it came to yours, mine, and ours. We chose not to have children, but our attitude was to level the financial jungle the best we could. College funds

and the parental expectations we held on that issue were very tough. With seven kids between us and the help that we could realistically offer, we quickly realized we needed to lower our expectations. For me as a dad, I wanted to help everyone, but funds were very limited. I felt if I could not do that for my own kids, how could I extend financial benefits to any of my new kids.

We told our kids that when it came to college, we would help with books the best we could. If they were ever hungry, they could come by and load up a shopping bag of food from the pantry or freezer. The door was always open. If a tank of gas would help too, we'd be there.

The choices the kids made from there were in their court. For us, this was tough. Yet in these financial times, even if we were both in our previous families, writing a check for $50,000–$100,000 for each of our bio kids to go to college…well, it just wasn't possible. One benefit was the fact that our ex's lived in the metro area close to our home so the kids were able to take advantage of both biological parents being close at hand.

Of course there was child support that came in one door and out the other. When it came to extra clothes or an activity, we did our best to cover them. Being able to do "extra" is something we budgeted into what we called the "kid account," because without fail, some odd expense would come up that we wanted to be able to address.

Adult Children and Money

When it comes to money issues with adult children, good communication is the key. Keeping short accounts with your kids will deflate any growing tensions or manipulations of inheritance or other financial issues. In the book *Money and Marriage God's Way,*[3] Howard Dayton of Crown Financial lays out step by step what you should do when you remarry with older kids. You may need to change the beneficiaries of your life insurance policies or change the ownership of car titles or deeds to a home or other property. New wills should also be drafted to reflect your changing circumstances.

As much as you may need to put any financial conflict from your kids to rest, you need to be mindful of your financial future as well. When speaking to your adult children about money issues, it's best to do it together, as a couple. You are showing that these are "we" decisions and that you are a united front.

The following are some bottom line pointers and options about money matters for stepfamilies:

Don'ts

1. Don't create two separate families under one roof. (Remember we're all on the same team, behind the same wall!)

2. Don't favor bio vs. stepkids, or vice versa. (This is a surefire way to divide the family, not conquer.)

3. Don't give your ex extra money that is beyond what the court ruled. (Unless your wife/husband fully supports this.)

4. Don't feel guilty and go overboard with the spoiling factor. (Buying your child's love will teach them unhealthy relationship skills and will affect their self-worth.)

Do's

1. Be 100 percent honest with any kind of money dealings. (You're not only shortchanging yourself but your family.)

2. Discuss your family/previous relationship of origin openly with your spouse. (This isn't to judge or degrade. It will give you some background information to understand certain thought and emotional processes.)

3. Live as one! (Everything is in one account and used as needed.)

4. Keep separate accounts if conflict can not be resolved. (As long as you both agree, sometimes this works; we prefer keeping one account. Pay for his/her self, his/her kids but

discuss total household/life expenses, such as vacations, clothes, activities, so there is no favoritism.)

5. Discuss imbalance of incoming "gifts' from the ex. (You and your spouse discuss with the ex how jealousies within the household can be minimized.)

6. Plan for your future. (You may have to start financially from square one. Be as aggressive as you can to save for your new family's future.)

Sex and money are definite hot buttons in a remarriage. It is common that these areas of your marriage will have their own unique ways of attacking your wall. They may be packaged differently, but they are still attacks. We don't mean to sound freaked out about this. Instead, we just want to raise your awareness pertaining to anything that will come against your wall. I (Brenda) find incredible comfort and strength in our wall. And when Gil and I are on the same page in these emotionally charged areas, there is nothing that can come between us.

Do your best to keep your checkbook out of the red.

As for the sheets, if they are red satin, wash them first! (And don't mix them with the rest of the wash!)

End of Chapter Questions

1. How are you doing in the foreplay department? How can you improve?

   _____

   _____

   _____

2. Have you prayed for the physical part of your relationship? If you haven't, what would you pray?

   _____

   _____

   _____

RESTORED & Remarried

3. Ladies, when was the last time you bought a new nightie? Guys, you
   can buy one for her too!

   _____

   _____

   _____

4. Has pornography intruded into your bedroom? If so, has it helped
   or hurt your relationship? Let's be honest here!

   _____

   _____

   _____

5. Since trust is the foundation for a good sex life, are there any Open
   Doors, Sneaker Waves, or Bare Wires that need to be shared?
   (Please be careful here. Only share the issues that are relevant in
   your relationship now.)

   _____

   _____

   _____

6. On a scale of 1-10 (1 being low and 10 being high) where are you as
   a couple with money issues? Where can you improve?

   _____

   _____

   _____

7. In your relationship, are there any Short Accounts that need to be addressed in this area of money management? Offer a safe place to share with each other.

_____

_____

_____

8. Where are you with the issue of money and kids? Is there good communication among all parties involved? Is the discussion age appropriate for each child?

_____

_____

_____

Action Item:

Have you made time to look at your financial future?

"Love is blind, but marriage restores its sight."

—George C. Lichtenberg

Restored & Remarried

Chapter 10

Preventing Another Derailment

RESTORED &
Remarried

Chapter 10

Preventing Another Derailment

Keep your train moving and on the right track

No one intends to endure another divorce when they remarry, ending up stuck in a place that leads to an emotional, financial, and often a physical train wreck. Our hope is to leave you with concepts that can be applied immediately in your remarriage relationship. As stated earlier, if you don't get these concepts and terms in place, it can leave the door open for major conflicts and strife.

One remarkable email we received just as we began to write this book has kept our noses to the grindstone and fingers to the laptop keys. We'll share just a bit of the email which we've held nearby for inspiration:

"We had just wed when taking your class at Northlake Christian in 2007—it was one of the most profound seminars we have ever taken. Specifically—I don't think we have ever put instructions (not including the Bible) to practice like we have yours. Thank you."

This very kind note came from a woman and her new husband who expressed how helpful terms like Bare Wires and concepts about "rocks in kid's buckets" had been to them and their remarriage. As remarried newlyweds with children who travel between two countries, she closed her email by stating that our ministry was powerful and imperative! All we could do was take a deep breath, accept the gratitude, and then press forward. Because of the "foxholes" we have been through, we wanted to write from our heart's experience to encourage you.

Our aim is to leave you with helpful concepts and terms that will assist you in successfully navigating through the minefield of remarriage and stepfamily life. Most importantly, the principles that influence you towards "right living" through Christ are our highest goal.

The message toward "right living" can only come with a proper understanding of who Christ is and what He provides to make uprightness possible. With all due respect, as I (Gil) listen to public

> *One of the most profound seminars we have ever taken.*

officials, counselors, attorneys, and social workers—even pastors—the secular idea that therapy or group sessions can fix people's problems is stated constantly. I agree that modern research has uncovered mountains of data that if practiced will change a person's life and relationships. Unfortunately, knowledge alone is not the most useful

change agent in social science. It has to be applied.

A friend of mine, who serves in our local district attorney's office and deals with drug rehab cases, shared a statistic that is worth noting. He said that if knowledge is not mixed with faith and God, the results are 20 percent to 30 percent effective for drug or alcohol recovery. The results jumped to 70 percent to 80 percent where faith in Christ, mixed with forgiveness, caused a change of heart and soul.

> *This book is empty unless you've come to a point of submission to Christ for your life as well as for your marriage.*

If that's the case with chemical dependency, why don't we get better results with our relationships? There are a myriad of marriage relationship/self-help books, so wouldn't you think that marriages would be stronger? What difference will it make to offer terms and concepts if a person's heart is not changed at the foundation?

Remember the foundation of the wall? It consists of two primary building blocks. You have total choice over both of them. You can choose to stay committed to your marriage...or not. You can choose to keep your faith in Christ...or not. Faith in Christ brings His strength to change you and rebuild you from the inside out.

Restoration is His part of the wall-building process. It is produced by your faith that He will do what no one else can. You need to establish forgiveness for yourself personally and find peace and dependence

upon His promises. Those bricks that were bruised, broken, and battered were much like the fabric of your life that ended in a heap, like the walls of Jerusalem after the dust settled.

When Christ is accepted and understood, He goes to work on your mind, soul, and heart. Here are four "C's" to remind you of His work:

1. Christ will lovingly act as a *convicting* instrument that will lead to steps of repentance (an about-face in direction and actions), thereby turning a person to a new way of life.

2. Christ will serve as a *convincing* teacher so that our hearts and intellect will behave in a new way of life with skills that follow His character.

3. Christ will fulfill a *covenant* whereby our primary relationships are anchored for the long haul because of His work on the cross.

4. Finally, Christ will walk along with you. He will lead you while *conquering* life's most stressful and defeating issues. By faith He will lift you successfully, not just for the here and now, but for eternity with Him!

This book is empty unless you've come to a point of submission to Christ for your life as well as for your marriage.

The warnings of Scripture caution us to not fall into pragmatic thinking, but be led by the Gospel, better known as the Good News of Grace, provided by Christ. A good marriage can grow from a broken or lost past. It can take something that ended in tragedy—a direct result of the many ideas and concepts followed by earthly wisdom—and turn it into something great.

A GREAT marriage—yes a great one—is truly possible. With Christ's grace restoring you from past errors, pride, selfishness, and other gods you've placed before Him, you can find that true restoration and joy.

By accepting His grace and provision for your life and new marriage, you can be set free from past patterns that were destructive, both to you and those around you. Your ability found in reliance upon His promises will make you watchful to not accept cheap grace and fall to selfishness. The more you surrender to Him, the more strength and confidence will grow as a settled assurance within your inner being.

He will build you up and restore your inheritance. His life in you will affect eternity, as well as the here and now! Your inheritance right now will be a restored family legacy—a family who truly understands restoration and grace.

Here is what one of our kids shared (age seventeen when we got married, twenty-three and married now):

> *"The marriage of my mom to Gil is evidence to me that the Gospel it true. The Gospel being, God in His mercy choosing to love a totally depraved sinful creation deserving of death, by the offering of His Son Jesus on a cross in our place; that through man's faith in Christ, God can redeem the human experience.*
>
> *If you have endured a divorce, I do not think it will be difficult, regardless of your faith, to be convinced of the evil that is within us human beings. Ask the husband whose wife has left him after twenty-five years, bitter and angry, wanting nothing to do with him (or men for that matter). Ask the wife whose husband left her and her three sons to go clubbing and relive his twenties. Ask the thirteen-year-old boy who rubs his mother's crying back attempting to comfort her in a loss he has no control over. These people, and people like them, have had a front-row seat to the fallen human condition.*
>
> *Some may ask, 'Where was God in that time?' or 'Where is God now?' God is mourning alongside you. You see, God knows firsthand what it was like to be betrayed by the one who kisses you. God knows what it is like to hear the venomous words by the ones He thought close. And God knows what it is like to have His bride, the Church, cheat on Him day in and day out. For this He died on a filthy*

roman cross.

But this is a story of redemption—where a Creator outside of His creation intervenes in the human experience. Having died—perfect, sinless, and without blemish—in our place for our sins, Jesus resurrects to new life . . . literally. And without this we have no hope. It is those who put their faith in the work of Christ that can experience true redemption, and God restores what is broken and heals what is wounded.

I can see the Gospel alive and well as God has brought together Mom and Gil. Two sinners in their own right, having been sinned against and left, God restores. Bringing them together, covenanting as one, washing them and the story of its sin for His glory! It is for our worship of God that this happens before our eyes. There are still scars on all of us, and prayers are still lifted for the betrayers. But where we are today is a miracle!

This is not the story of all blended families. Our blended family works, not because of good communication skills and acronyms, although helpful. It is our identity in Jesus, being a part of His family, and our worship of Him that makes this a reality. Apart from Christ, the cycles of sin could be at work destroying each one. What God has done for us is for you to see and experience what is possible, only in and through hope and faith in Jesus. This is how I tell the story of my blended family."

We have covered a lot of ground in the previous chapters. Here is a quick review:

Chapter 1

Restored Foundations, Adjusted Expectations, Misleading Myths

Take some time, if you haven't already, to assess where you are with the restoration process. Are there people in your life that you need to forgive? How about yourself? Acknowledge the myths you may have

fallen into and replace them with trust and honesty for yourself and your family. Above all, pray! Remember, it affects the bedroom.

Chapter 2

The Wall

ROI—Return on Investment. What does your emotional balance sheet look like regarding relationships in your life? As uncomfortable as it might be, ask for encouragement or help. Please do not isolate yourself or your family. Ask for help. Your situation may not be as bad as you think. Relationship and family "tools" will help keep your wall strong. Check on the condition of your mortar (safety) in your wall from time to time. Have fun creating new acrostics for your wall!

Chapter 3

"I Didn't Think It Was Going to Be Like This"

Are you committed to your spouse and your family? If not, time to "man up" (ladies too). "I'm not going anywhere" can bring strength and confidence to your relationship. If it helps, say it out loud! Do you have a Cabo experience to share? Share Open Doors and Bare Wires, then practice your listening skills, daily!

Chapter 4

"I Didn't See This Coming"

Have you scheduled a "Triple F Night"? You can do this even if your kids are adults! Have you implemented any of these terms in your relationship? Sneaker Waves, Old Tapes/New Tapes, Foxholes, Phantoms, and Short Accounts. If not these terms, we encourage you to create your own! Remember, it's the little things that destroy a relationship and it's the little things that can make a relationship.

Chapter 5

Those People

How are your relationships with Those People? Don't forget to put

yourself in their shoes once in awhile. Crockpot cooking is best. Don't be a target of isolation. The enemy can take you out! Have you gone on a date with your stepchild(ren) yet? Have you complimented them lately?

Chapter 6

Parenting

Are you being the dad/mom you would want? No matter how your ex is acting in your co-parenting relationship, you can only change yourself! Have you cut and cauterized where needed? Have you been able to apologize for rocks in your kids' buckets? What about anyone else's buckets? Keep the load light!

Chapter 7

Two Countries and an Elephant

If picking up and dropping off your kids is part of your life right now, how is the transfer process? Is it similar to a POW swap? Have you had any family meetings lately? When was the last time you heard your child speak from the heart? Start talking about the holidays now. What new traditions can you start? You can never go wrong adding history to your family and its legacy.

Chapter 8

Teens, Adult Children, and Grandparents

Teenagers need independence, yet they also need encouragement to connect with the family. Lower your expectations with adult stepchildren, but make efforts to reach out. Have you acknowledged any relatives in your family who may need reassurance from the grief they have experienced because of your divorce/remarriage? It might be interesting to ask your kids to write their experience about the remarriage. As time has gone by, it has been very insightful to us (the parents) to hear how they have viewed our changing family—the good, the bad, and the ugly!

Chapter 9

Sex and Money

Keep creativity flowing when it comes to the sexual part of your relationship. Both of you are responsible for keeping the flame of passion going strong. Guard your thought life. If pornography is an issue, eliminate if from your life. It's not worth it . . . really! Talk about your likes and dislikes regarding your sex life. In the bedroom, use the terms we have introduced (Sneaker Waves, Bare Wires, etc.). Above all, be honest! Especially in the money department. You're on the same team, remember?

Don't Fight Naked

Our culture is bent on the destruction of the sanctity of marriage. This really is a battle. As a society we have accepted the norms of no-fault divorce, co-habitation, and gay marriage. According to Linda Waite and Maggie Galagher, authors of *The Case for Marriage*, the marriage contract is less binding than the average business deal.[1]

You've lived through the crisis of divorce. You've been a statistic. Now do something to fight for your family legacy and to impact your community where you live. Don't fight naked. Ephesians 6:13-18 reminds us *"to put on the armor of God"*:

> *"Therefore take up the full armor of God, that you may be able to resist in the evil day, and having done everything, to stand firm. Stand firm therefore, having girded your loins with truth, and having put on the breastplate of righteousness, and having shod your feet with the preparation of the gospel of peace; in addition to all, taking up the shield of faith, with which you will be able to extinguish all the flaming missiles of the evil one. And take the helmet of salvation, and the sword of the Spirit, which is the word of God. With all prayer and petition pray at all times in the Spirit, and with this in view, be on the alert with all perseverance and petition for all the saints."*

What will the armor of God look like on a daily basis in the intricacies of our lives and remarriages? Here are a few thoughts:

- Belt of truth

  "...and you shall know the truth, and the truth shall set you free." **John 8:32**

  Accept the truth of the Gospel because of what Christ did on the cross. Trust and honesty with God are number one! He can handle it. You are just fooling yourself if you think you can hide anything from Him. There isn't anything He doesn't already know. There is too much at stake now with your stepfamily to play any games with each other. Operating in the mode of trust and honesty will make life run a lot smoother and cleaner. Short accounts are essential here! You owe it to each other and your family.

- Breastplate of righteousness/integrity

  "Let us therefore lay aside the deeds of the darkness and put on the armor of light..." **Romans 13:12**

  Character. What kind do you have? What would other people say about you? Using Christ as our standard for how to conduct ourselves is both challenging and revealing. Some areas of our life will be easier than others. When the Light reveals those weaker areas of our lives, we have a choice as to what we are going to do. We either continue in ignorance or meet the areas head on. Are you prepared to "clean out the corners of your house"? Open Doors will allow you to be transparent with your spouse to help identify these areas. Revisiting the concepts of confession, redemption, and repentance will help keep you in line with the Father. Forgiving yourself and others is another vital step in the chiseling out of character. The ultimate goal is to be a man/woman of integrity and righteousness . . . let Christ help!

- Feet shod with the Gospel of peace

"How lovely on the mountains are the feet of him who brings good news, who announces peace and brings good news of happiness..." **Isaiah 52:7**

"Shod" means "prepared" with the Gospel of peace. Operating in defensiveness and suspicion in our home just leaves a foothold for the enemy. If our objective is to have close supporting relationships within our blended family (which it should), we need to have an aroma of peace in our home. We still need to speak truth and not sugarcoat situations. Will there be peace all the time? Maybe not, and that's OK. As long as the underlying theme of peace is in our home, like a brick in your wall, a temporary unsettledness may need to happen to flush out feelings. If Bare Wires are being hit, even among the kids, let's call it what it is and work through it!

> *The marriage contract is less binding than the average business deal.*

- Shield of faith

"The Lord is my strength and my shield." **Psalm 28:7**

"...knowing that the testing of your faith produces endurance." **James 1:3**

Living in this world, we **will** be attacked spiritually. There is no getting around it. Knowing this, why are we so surprised when bad things happen? If you think about it, we should be more surprised when we're not under attack! Life is tough; it feels like an endurance test at times! Take the quiet moments to take advantage of polishing your armor and getting ready for the next round! We need to do the same with our wall. The wall that we use as a shield for our marriages and families needs to be kept in good repair. Some bricks may have had some major hits and need attention. It is vital to keep our faith strong in Jesus Christ, who ultimately keeps our marriage wall up. Our faith and trust in Him should hold us to a high standard in our marriage to stay committed and strong. Have confidence and hope in Him.

> *Putting your armor on is a choice. Keeping it on is a challenge.*

- Helmet of salvation

"And do not be conformed to this world, but be transformed by the renewing of your mind, that you may prove what the will of God is, that which is good and acceptable and perfect." **Romans 12:2**

Merriam-Webster's Dictionary describes a helmet as: *any of various protective head coverings usually made of a hard material to resist impact.*

Garbage in, garbage out. What images and thoughts are you putting into your head? Do not underestimate their power. Protecting our mind and thoughts is our responsibility to our marriage and family. Remember, no back doors. No "D" word. Even uttering the word "divorce" opens that door in your relationship. Hold yourself and each other accountable to eliminate Old Tapes that will get in the way of this new

incredible relationship (even if you've been remarried awhile). Create those New Tapes in your mind and practice them. We're using DVDs and Blu-ray now, right? Keeping Philippians 4:8 in mind is also important: *"Finally brethren, whatever is true, whatever is honorable, whatever is right, whatever is of good repute, if there is any excellence and if anything worthy of praise, let your mind dwell on these things."*

- Sword of the Spirit (the Word of God)

"For the word of God is living and active and sharper than any two-edged sword, and piercing as far as the division of soul and spirit, of both joints and marrow, and able to judge the thoughts and intentions of the heart." **Hebrews 4:12**

There is power in His Word. This is part of our armor that we need to put on every day. I (Brenda) must admit, I fall short in this area. My intentions are there, but I don't always follow through, holding a specific Scripture in mind throughout my day. I share this to encourage you. I know that I am not the only one who may fall short here. And I know the Lord knows this too. Yet I understand the power that the Word holds and I am cheating myself for not taking full advantage of it. So, I challenge you too. Pick a Scripture and hold it close so that it can permeate every area of your heart and mind. When I slow down enough to do that, He does incredible things in my life. It boils down to a choice. I can choose to dwell on His word or make other priorities. OK, have I preached enough yet? When you are in the Foxholes of life, Scripture will bring confidence and hope. Wielding that sword as a couple makes your marriage invincible. Use the Word to protect and defend your marriage and family.

- Pray at all times

You may have seen this before. It is a great tool to use when it comes time to pray:

A Adoration to our Lord

C Confess your sins to Him

T Thanksgiving for what He has done for you and what He will do in and through you

S Supplication is where you stand in the gap for a person or situation

This acronym is a great reminder of how to pray. It's not meant to be legalistic, but can be a refreshing way to connect with our Father when we get in a rut of praying the same old way. Christ wants the best for us. Knowing His heart for us can be comforting and encouraging at the same time, especially when the fiery arrows of life come against our wall (because they will). Praying with your spouse is very intimate. Please do not miss this chance to connect with each other spiritually. It will bring a depth to your relationship that will put it at a different level and will drive the foundation of your wall to unfathomable depths. Be quiet, be still and listen. He is waiting for you.

Putting your armor on is a choice. Keeping it on is a challenge. Remember the 60/80 rule? Having people in your life to help you stand strong is imperative. Don't do this alone! On another note, you have no idea how Christ can use you and your story to help someone else. All He asks of you is to show up and be available. Let Him do the rest.

Here are some suggestions:

- If you are not aware of a small group for stepfamilies, start one. Even if it's just with one couple to encourage one another. We have an eight-week study guide available for you to use as a couple or in a small group. It's very user friendly and will help build community.

- On a larger scale, find out about marriage and family initiatives in your city and in your county. We are involved

with Thriving Families of Clark County, part of Families Northwest/Stronger Families. We are involved with community events that help strengthen marriages and families and Community Marriage covenants. Check out your local area.

Last Brick for Your Wall

ENJOY. It's one final acrostic that we'd like to share with our readers, and it has a story behind its formation. Recently, when pulling together memories and keepsakes for our upcoming anniversary, I (Gil) came across a folder of photos that I presented to Brenda during our wedding ceremony.

A first for her and me.

The scene was set with her walking down the aisle with her dad, who by the way did **not** walk her down the aisle for her first wedding ceremony. I was so honored that her father actually gave her away to me and no one else. That act alone was a first for her and me which was a huge deal to both of us that evening. (Thanks, Norm, you are one cool father-in-law.)

The little chapel was calm, yet festive, as we progressed through the songs and Scripture reading portion of the ceremony. We even did a short dance—with a dip—after we both arrived on stage at the beginning introductions. The audience applauded and celebrated with us, as many knew our stories.

Just before we were to finish with the "I do's" and "I will's" and "I promise"—which preceded the words "you may kiss your bride"—I had a plan prearranged with Brenda. I wanted to serve my wife from the beginning of our marriage.

What happened next caused the women to cry and the men who were in attendance to hate me. I had our favorite love song played, "Pour Your Love on Me" by Phillips, Craig & Dean. While it played, I had Brenda sit in a chair while I slipped my tux jacket off and tossed it to our pastor who was officiating the ceremony. I knelt in front of her and pulled from a box a basin large enough for her feet to rest in. I had a warm jug of water nearby, along with some fancy lotion and rubbing oils for her feet, which I washed while the music played.

Knowing the length of the music plus the sentiment of the words, I had taken the entire day before the ceremony to trace back to significant locations during our courtship and take photos. The pictures were

> *What happened next caused the women to cry and the men to hate me.*

placed in the folder and were numbered in order of where we went on our first date up to the location where I asked Brenda to marry me.

The lyrics to the song told of what an incredible friend she was to me and the love that I wished to pour out on her. (Did I tell you I served her a glass of wine too while the music played, since that was part of the lyrics as well?) While she sat there, she worked her way through the photos and the wine, dabbing her eyes with a hankie.

And Gil has not stopped serving me (Brenda) to this day! Thanks honey!

The final page in the folder was the acrostic we wish to share with you now. It is the word *Enjoy*. Create your own ENJOY acrostic.

E Enthusiastic

N Never ending

J Journey

O Overflowing through the

Y Years

The foundation of Christ's redemption and forgiveness should be established first in your life and marriage. In order for marriage and family to be restored and enjoyed, we must first understand the current condition of these vital institutions. Remarriage and stepfamilies are very fragile. They need to have intentional communication, grace, understanding, and patience. Commitment has to be 100 percent. There will be trials where you must gather strength from behind your wall. Then arm yourself with information and supportive relationships for your remarriage to succeed. Together you can not only have a good stepfamily, but you can have a great stepfamily by remembering…

If you ain't got the marriage, you ain't got nothin'.

Appendix

Stepfamily Resources

- *Restored and Remarried* by Gil and Brenda Stuart
  www.restoredandremarried.com

- Building a Successful Stepfamily
  The Smart Stepfamily by Ron Deal
  www.successfulstepfamilies.com

- Blending a Family
  God Breathes on Blended Families by Moe and Paige Becnel
  www.blendingafamily.com

- Rebuilding Families
  www.rebuildingfamilies.net
  Blended Families by Maxine Marsolini
  Raising Children in Blended Families by Maxine Marsolini

- *Designing Dynamic Stepfamilies* by Gordon and Carri Taylor
  www.designingdynamicstepfamilies.com

- InStep Ministries—Jeff and Judi Parziale
  www.instepministries.com

- Changing Families
  www.changingfamilies.com

- *Laugh Your Way to a Better Marriage* by Mark Gungor
  www.laughyourway.com
  www.flagpage.com

- Real Relationships
  Saving Your Second Marriage Before It Starts by Drs. Les and
  Leslie Parrott
  www.realrelationships.com

- *Stepfamily Survival Guide* by Natalie Gillespie

- *The Good Divorce* by Dr. Constance Ahrons
  www.constanceahrons.com

- Stronger Families (formally Families Northwest)
  www.strongerfamilies.org

- Crown Financial (finances)
  www.crown.org

- Dave Ramsey (financial)
  www.daveramsey.com

Endnotes

Scripture quotations are taken from the Ryrie Study Bible, New American Standard Translation, Copyright 1976, 1978 by the Moody Bible Institute.

Introduction

1. US Census Bureau, 2006

2. US Census Bureau, 2006

Chapter 1

Epigraph. Jerry Cook, quoted in "Marriage Quotes," The Coalition for Marriage, Family, and Couples Education, http://www.smartmarriages.com/marriage.quotes.html

1. US Census Bureau, 2006

2. US Census Bureau, 2006

3. Mark Gungor, "Laugh Your Way to a Better Marriage" live presentation Clark County Mayor and Leaders Prayer Breakfast, Vancouver, WA, 2006. Presentation title: "Getting it Right."

4. Ron L. Deal, *Building a Successful Step-Family: Encouragement, Wisdom, and Compassion for Puzzling Times* (FamilyLife, 2001). Workbook/studyguide available at www.successfulstepfamilies.org/stepfamily.

5. Prepare and Enrich marriage/couple relationship inventory product of Life Innovations, Inc. Minneapolis, MN. Go to www.prepare-enrich.com for more information.

6. Stu Weber, *The Heart of a Tender Warrior* (Sisters, OR: Multnomah Publishers Inc., 2002).

7. E. Mavis Hetherington and John Kelly, *For Better or for Worse: Divorce Reconsidered* (New York, NY: W.W. Norton & Company, Inc., 2002).

Chapter 2

1. US Census Bureau, 2006.

2. Lists to Live by for Every Married Couple, compiled by Dr. Steve Stephens, Alice Gray and John Van Diest (Sisters, OR: Multnomah Publishers, 2001).

Chapter 3

Epigraph. Simone Signoret, quoted in Jewish Women's Archive, http://jwa.org/encyclopedia/article/signoret-simone.

1. Autumn Ray, "Marriage Team" a personal quote during Marriage Coach training, Summer 2007. www.marriageteam.org.

2. Drs. Les and Leslie Parrott, *Saving Your Second Marriage Before It Starts* (Grand Rapids, MI: Zondervan, 2001).

3. Moe and Page Becnel, *God Breathes on Blended Families* (Baton Rouge, LA: Healing Place Productions, 2000).

4. Ron L. Deal, *The Smart Stepfamily* (Bloomington, MN: Bethany House Publishers, 2002).

5. John Eldredge and Brent Curtis, *The Sacred Romance* (Nashville, TN: Thomas Nelson, 1997).

6. John Eldredge, *Wild at Heart* (Nashville, TN: Thomas Nelson: 2001).

7. Mark Gungor offers live video presentations or DVDs of "Laugh Your Way to a Better Marriage." Visit www.laughyourway.com for more information.

Chapter 4

Epigraph. ThinkExist.com, "Louis K. Anspacher Quotes," http://thinkexist.com/quotation/marriage_isthatrelationbetween man and woman/254219.html.

1. Emerson Eggerichs, *Love and Respect* (Nashville, TN: Integrity Publishers, 2004). http://www.loveandrespect.com/

2. Gary Chapman, *The Five Love Languages* (Chicago: Moody, 1995).

Chapter 5

1. Ron L. Deal, *The Smart Stepfamily* (Bloomington, MN: Bethany House Publishers, 2002) 70.

2. Flag Page, created by Larry Biolotta and used by Mark Gungor during Laugh Your Way to a Better Marriage seminars. Go to www.flagpage.com for more information.

3. The names in this story have been changed.

4. Mike McManus, "Marriage Savers Answers 25 Tough Questions," http://www.marriagesavers.org/sitems/Resources/Articles/Art007TwentyFiveQuestions.htm

5. Judith Wallerstein is a psychologist and researcher who has devoted twenty-five years to the study of the long-term effects of divorce. (See http://www.divorceinfo.com/judithwallerstein.htm for more information.)

6. Judith Wallerstein, quoted in Mike McManus, "Marriage Savers Answers 25 Tough Questions," http://www.marriagesavers.org/sitems/Resources/Articles/Art007TwentyFiveQuestions.htm

7. Ron L. Deal, *Building a Successful Stepfamily: Encouragement, Wisdom, and Compassion for Puzzling Times* (FamilyLife: 2001). This audio seminar and workbook is available at http://www.successfulstepfamilies.com/stepfamily.

Chapter 6

Epigraph. Brainy Quote, "Robert Fulghum Quotes." http://www.brainyquote.com/quotes/authors/r/robert_fulghum.html.

1. *The Journal of Biblical Counseling*, Vol. 16, No. 2, Winter 1998.

2. Moe and Paige Becnel, *God Breathes on Blended Families* ibid.

3. Constance Ahrons, *The Good Divorce* (New York, NY: HarperCollins, 1998).

4. Elizabeth Einstein and Linda Albert, *Strengthening Your Stepfamily* (Atascadero, CA: Impact Publishers, Inc., 2005).

Chapter 7

1. Dynamic Stepfamilies is an eight-week stepfamily seminar consisting of facilitated video conferences from seasoned stepfamily professionals Gordon and Carri Taylor. Visit http://www.designingdynamicstepfamilies.com/ for more information.

Chapter 8

1. Guttmacher Institute, "U.S. Teenage Pregnancy Statistics, National Trends and Trends by State and Ethnicity." http://www.guttmacher.org/pubs/2006/09/12/USTPstats.pdf.

2. NCPTP, "Why It Matters." http://www.thenationalcampaign.org/why-it-matters/pdf/risky_behaviors.pdf.

3. National Institute on Drug Abuse, "Marijuana: Facts for Teens". http://www.theantidrug.com.

4. Illusions: Uncovering the Truth About Pornography, "Stuff to Think About." http://www.illusionsprogram.net/commercial-stuff-to-think-about.html.

5. Kaiser Family Foundation, "Number of Sexual Scenes on TV Nearly Double Since 1998." http://www.kff.org/entmedia/entmedia110905nr.cfm.

6. NCPTP, With One Voice: America's Adults and Teens Sound Off About Teen Pregnancy, Washington, DC: National Campaign to Prevent Teen Pregnancy, 2002.

Chapter 9

1. Ginger Kolbaba's, *Surprised by Remarriage: A Guide to the Happily-Even-After* (Grand Rapids, MI: Revell, 2006).

2. Mark Gungor offers live video presentations or DVDs of "Laugh Your Way to a Better Marriage." Visit www.laughyourway.com for more information.

3. Howard Dayton, *Money and Marriage God's Way*, (Chicago: Moody, 2009).

Chapter 10

1. Linda Waite and Maggie Galagher, *The Case for Marriage* (New York, NY: Doubleday, 2000).

RESTORED & Remarried

ENCOURAGEMENT FOR REMARRIED COUPLES IN A STEPFAMILY

Pick Up Your Copy Of The Restored and Remarried Workbook

Your relationship faces many unique challenges. You'll find this eight-week workbook practical, encouraging, and a great resource for your stepfamily adventure.

Your struggles are directly addressed with content centering on the issues presented in the seminar and the *Restored & Remarried* book. In a small group setting, you'll have a guide as you dialogue with others around the terms and concepts related to remarriage and stepfamily life. This guide can also be used for "just the two of you."

You can never get enough support and encouragement in your marriage. We are honored to be part of your process of leaving a healthy, strong legacy for your family.

Workbooks can be purchased at the Restored and Remarried Seminar or by contacting us at www.restoredandremarried.com.

CPSIA information can be obtained
at www.ICGtesting.com
Printed in the USA
LVHW102352240723
753358LV00025B/166

9 780557 108527